W9-BDF-479

FROM THE LIBRARY OF

RICHARD CARPENTER

Leadership
in crisis

donald gerig

Regal
Books

A Division of G/L Publications
Ventura, CA U.S.A.

Other good reading:
Be a Leader People Follow by David L. Hocking
Reaching Your Possibilities Through Commitment by
  Gerald W. Marshall
Strategy for Living by Edward R. Dayton and Ted W.
  Engstrom

The foreign language publishing of all Regal books is under the direction of GLINT. GLINT provides financial and technical help for the adaptation, translation and publishing of books in more than 85 languages for millions of people worldwide.

For more information write: GLINT, P.O. Box 6688, Ventura, California 93006.

Scripture quotations in this publication are from the Authorized King James version of the Bible. Also quoted is the RSV, *Revised Standard Version* of the Bible, copyrighted 1946 and 1952 by the Division of Christian Education of the NCCC, U.S.A., and used by permission.

© Copyright 1981 by Regal Books
All rights reserved

Published by Regal Books
A Division of GL Publications
Ventura, California 93006
Printed in U.S.A.

Library of Congress Cataloging in Publication Data
Gerig, Donald, 1939-
    Leadership in crisis.

    Bibliography: p.
    1. Christian leadership. 2. Leadership.
I. Title.
BV652.1.G47   649'.7   81-51741
ISBN 0-8307-0797-2   AACR2

Contents

One

The Climate
for Leadership

It all started during one of those casual discussions with friends after a holiday meal. Our host's mother, who had spoken on many college campuses around the country, raised the question first. "Why are so many Christian kids reluctant to assert themselves and be leaders in their particular areas of specialty?" We had no statistical data to back up our suspicions, but it soon became apparent that evening that all of us were wrestling with that issue in one way or another. How could the flow of Christian leaders, people who could have a positive influence on the world around them, be increased?

The question came up again while I was having lunch one day with a prominent Christian leader. I discovered that he, too, was wrestling with this issue. His observation was, "Don, many Christian groups are better known for the leaders they have lost than for the leaders they have!"

As I began to do some preliminary study in this area, I ran across others who shared my concern. A president of one organization observed in a letter, "It seems strange that some of the more visible and effective leaders in our country are people who have come out of non-Christian and/or unbelieving backgrounds, have been converted, and then emerged in roles of leadership."

In his book, *Death in the City*, Francis Schaeffer observes that, "in the United States in the twenties not everyone was a Christian, but in general there was a Christian consensus. Now that consensus is completely gone."[1] He goes on to point out that the lost consensus is not only in terms of actual numbers of Christians but in the lack of influence on the culture by those who are Christians. This means Christians do not necessarily have to be in the majority to exert a Christian influence; a strategically placed minority can do it! In those times of history when the church had its greatest influence there were outstanding theologians and preachers, but even more importantly there were Christian teachers, artists, musicians, poets, philosophers, politicians . . . people who effected a positive influence on *all* of society.

What can we do to recapture that sort of initiative today? Are there ways by which we can produce an ever-increasing flow of leaders who are Christian into every legitimate discipline? I, for one, think there are!

What we must strive for is the creation of a "climate for leadership" in our Christian homes and institutions. If we think and act in ways that encourage the development of leaders, we will not have to artificially push people into leadership (or, worse, lose the battle for influence by default). Instead, leaders will naturally emerge from our ranks. But if, while we "pray the Lord of the harvest to send forth laborers into His harvest" (Luke 10:2), we are guilty of attitudes which discourage or defeat potential leaders, we have already insured that our own prayers will not be answered.

What Is Leadership?

What is "leadership" anyway? It is possible to make that definition too difficult. Webster, in a part of his definition, says that leadership is "that ingredient of personality which causes men to follow." Pretty simple, isn't it? But that comes very close to capturing the whole story.

It is true that there can be bad leaders or good ones. There can be selfish or unselfish leaders. But whether for good or ill, a leader is the one who is in front of others influencing those who follow. One of my seminary professors used to speak of the "3 percent who read *Time* magazine and influence the thinking of the other 97 percent." Obviously those figures could not stand the test of close examination, and the readers of *Newsweek* would argue vehemently over the choice of magazines, but the principle is still well taken. What that professor constantly sought to do was challenge Christians to be in that three percent category—people who influence others in their particular fields of endeavor.

With the resurgent prominence of evangelicals in the past few years, we have started to see a hopeful emergence of leaders committed to Jesus Christ. When, according to a 1977 poll by NBC News, one-third of the adult population in the United States claims to be "born again," we face a trend that starts to put the law of averages on the side of the Christian. Influence for good is now a possibility if in that "one-third" segment of the population there is included a corps of effective leaders. That is the concern of this book, to see that the climate is right for such leadership development!

Accepting the Challenge

The challenge of leadership development must be accepted by the Christian community at large. In our churches and institutions we must encourage attitudes that will encourage leadership development. We cannot afford the luxury of merely mouthing our agreement to the need for leaders. There will be times when current leaders will have to take a positive stand in support of new attitudes in the church which will encourage leaders to emerge. It may be that some organizations will have to courageously resist the pressure of constituent groups when those pressures diminish the opportunity for leaders to develop.

What this book will seek to do is identify several elements that are necessary in creating a climate for leadership development. It is my conviction that through a study of Scripture and human behavior we can identify some of the essential ingredients common to the background of leaders. Such a study should then challenge us to create a more precisely defined climate for leadership.

It must also be said that while the challenge for creating this leadership climate must be accepted by the Christian community at large, the primary battleground will be in individual Christian homes. It is true that churches and other institutions have an enormous effect on our children, but there is still nothing to substitute for what happens in the home. While this book makes no claim to be a manual on how to raise children, it will, without apology, seek to point out how the climate for leadership has to start in the home. There are factors in home life that will either help or hinder the chances for leaders to be developed.

I would particularly hope that this message will get through to homes where children are still young. Parents, grandparents, teachers, pastors—anyone who can have influence in homes with young children—should catch the importance of the constituent parts of the climate for leadership.

This need was brought home to me while I was visiting with a good friend who was involved for many years in education. He reiterated what I had heard before. "The crucial period has to be the first six years of a child's life," he said. "A lazy 2-year-old will probably become a lazy 10-year-old and later a lazy 30-year-old!" Family after family has crossed the threshold of my office to talk about the problems they are having with their teenagers. Popular conference speakers can pack auditoriums when they speak about the solution to teenage problems. But with disappointing frequency we have to say that it is almost too late for effective help at that point. So it will be with leadership development. From the day of birth we must see that the climate for leadership exists in our homes. Then we will see emerging leaders, not problems, when those children reach 18!

So, our adventure begins! We now start our search for those elements in our homes and institutions that will, when put together, create a climate for leadership. We must, because the stakes are high! As we succeed we will be able to be the "salt which has not lost its flavor" (see Matt. 5:13) in a world that needs the seasoning of the Christian. Leaders can again bear an influence for good in all legitimate vocations. God can be honored through that influence. And we will have the satisfaction of knowing that we kept open the chance for God to work through us and our children!

Two

Smother or Nourish

John Gardner, in his thought-provoking book, *Excellence*, effectively shatters one of our familiar myths: "If we accept the common usage of words, nothing can be more readily disproved than the old saw, 'You can't keep a good man down.' Most human societies have been beautifully organized to keep good men down."[2] I would add that most Christian homes and institutions have also been disappointingly proficient in keeping good men down.

Somewhere along the line a strange idea has developed that in order to be humble we also have to be mediocre. Spirituality and excellence are seen as opposite ends of a pole. Where we get this idea is a mystery. Certainly not from Scripture! Over and over God selected people marked by excellence for His work. Whether it was Moses of the Old Testament with his excellent heritage and palace training, or Paul in the New Testament with his excellent knowledge and organizational ability, God chose the best.

And He still does! Typical of what is happening in many places in the world is the experience of a friend of ours now working in Haiti. Having graduated with an agricultural degree and proven himself an effective agricultural authority in a farming situation, Sam felt God leading him to community development work in this needy land. Now, because of excellence in his work, literally thousands of people are being blessed with a new chance for life through ingenious self-help projects.

Just Existing

The enemy we fight in developing a climate of excellence is our natural tendency to "just get by." Left to ourselves we have a tendency to maintain a standard of excellence only high enough to exist. Why work so hard when a little less will do? All you need to do is ask the typical school child to work on an extra project to find this out. "Do I have to?" may be the response you will get. Or, "Will it give me a better grade?" To merely do something for the sake of becoming better seems so unnecessary in our society.

Another part of the "just existing" syndrome is our absorption of the all-American profit motive: If it is good enough to sell don't worry about making it better. By the same token, if the only thing that sells is that which compromises with excellence, so be it! It really is not too difficult to see where this leads in the search for excellence.

In church we sometimes hide the fact that we too sacrifice excellence for profit by changing the word profit to "results." It does sound more spiritual; however, much of the time it still leaves us short of our best. If people respond to a half-effort, it somehow seems to justify that half-effort. After all, weren't there results? How does this differ in the long run, though, from the world's idea that what sells is good enough?

I am not suggesting an artificial and arbitrary line of excellence. That would be risky because undoubtedly the line of excellence (if drawn in this arbitrary way) would end up being a line at my own level of excellence. Anyone doing as well as, or better than, I is doing his best, while everyone below my line would be guilty of just existing. The folly of that reasoning should be evident enough.

What we are talking about, however, is a separate line of excellence for each person. Am *I* doing all that *I* am capable of? This line of excellence includes every last person God has created. Excellence is just as valid a concept for a mentally retarded child as it is for the child prodigy with a brilliant IQ. No person needs to merely exist. No Christian needs to sell out to the idea that if it works it is good enough. If everyone is being challenged to do his best (whatever that may be for the specific individual), you can be certain that from that climate will come some who will be leaders making an impact in the world to the glory of God.

As I write these words I find myself reflecting on several people who have made a profound impact on my life through their ministry or their writings. None of them had great academic preparation for their work, but every one had obviously determined to work to their full potential. Because they would offer God only their best, they were all used widely in His service. They read widely, studied diligently, and thought profoundly. They refused to "just exist" and I, for one, am grateful to God for that fact!

Is Better Bad?

An honest mistake is still, unfortunately, a mistake! It is undoubtedly an honest mistake to infer that better is bad. We really have not thought through the issue as we should. We even sing, "Give of your best to the Master!" But in practice we often fall very short of that goal. Perhaps it is because, in some subtle way, we have accepted the idea that better is bad.

For some it starts with a misunderstanding of what it means to be "equal" in Christ. There is no doubt that we come before Him with an equal need. Of course it is true that His grace is available to us equally. Yes, God loves each of us as we are in equal portion. But why does it follow that any person should be embarrassed about being better than another in a particular endeavor? Why should I shy away from developing my talents and gifts to the best of my ability even if it means excelling over other Christians?

Certainly in Scripture there were those who excelled. Solomon chose Hiram to do all the bronze work for the Temple because he was a skilled craftsman; he was better than everyone else! Paul chose Timothy because he had promise of being a better leader than others. And he encouraged Timothy to pursue that excellence (see 1 Tim. 4:14; 2 Tim. 2:15).

Excellence is not something given to us like a gift. It is not a quality we have or don't have at birth. You don't stumble into it. Rather, excellence comes from discipline and purpose and work.

Recently friends of ours took us to the Lambs' Farm near Chicago. This farm is a work center for mentally retarded adults. What struck me throughout the tour was the mark of excellence on every piece of work done there. From the pet shop to the printing shop to the bakery, the work was of the highest quality. The equipment used was the best. Here, obviously, were people who never accepted the adage that better is bad. And the instructors had drawn excellence out of a community of people that many of us might have written off as having no potential.

Has it ever occurred to you how incongruous it must seem to our children when they are encouraged to sing about giving their best to the Master in a service where the hymn is printed in a bulletin that was obviously thrown together in haste, when the hymn is sung in a church that was built with leftovers and cheap seconds, when those who teach the church give little evidence of having studied with any diligence at all, when those same teachers poke fun at the "big shots" in big churches? How can we help but communicate the idea that better must be bad?

I remember talking with an individual who did a great deal of speaking to Christian groups on college campuses. She expressed to me that her greatest frustration was the number of Christian students who could have been real leaders in many different disciplines but instead hung back because they seemed embarrassed about being better than others.

Our standard will prove to be contagious. If we convey the notion that better is bad, we will see that idea spread to our children. Our churches will be affected. By the same token, if we can encourage excellence, that too will spread. Why not recognize those who excel! Why not set the pattern for excellence in everything we do! Is better bad? The answer from the lips of a Christian should be a resounding NO!

Excellence for Whose Sake?

In dealing with the concept of excellence we must talk about motivation. It is at this point that excellence often gets bad press among us. It does not take long to discover that those who do strive for excellence sometimes do it for the wrong reasons. And, naturally, Christians have a tendency to recoil from bad motivations.

I recall my disillusionment as a college student as I overheard a conversation between members of an evangelistic team. The discussion centered around how to "spruce up the act" in order to make a big impression at an upcoming engagement. The reason? So their fame would spread and they could land an even bigger engagement on the horizon! That was not the reason given in public, of course, but from that overheard conversation I have to assume it was the true one. Coming as it did at a time when I had been taught that one should be suspicious of success, that incident did nothing to spur me on to excellence!

By happy contrast there came a time when that bad impression was corrected in a community evangelistic effort in which I cooperated. Again, I heard the challenge from this evangelistic team for excellence. I worked on the inside of the planning and preparation for that crusade, and I saw how the excellence was really a significant factor in making a positive impact for God on the community.

What was the difference? The glory of God! In one case excellence was for the glory of man; in the other, the glory of God. As one good friend put it to me over lunch one day, "True excellence should proceed from true worship!"

Parents certainly must struggle with this issue. Sometimes it seems terribly difficult to distinguish between encouraging excellence in our children for God's glory and for our own. As we will mention again in other chapters, there is a great temptation for parents to live their lives through the lives of their children.

The result is often a nagging, selfish approach to the raising of children. Even apart from the consideration of God's will and glory, it makes little sense for parents to push for excellence for their own glory. Rudolf Dreikurs has pointed out that the "pedagogical benefits of nagging are nil."[3] He goes on to show how such nagging often backfires. Instead of producing the child prodigy from whom we can gain esteem as parents, we tend to strengthen the child's resistance and actually encourage his failure.

Does that mean that we dare not encourage our children to excellence—to doing their best? Not at all! But it must really be for the right reason—for the glory of God!

This is, admittedly, dangerous ground. Some Christian writers honestly feel that pushing a child for even good reasons carries too much risk. They feel that the dangers of frustrating a child by trying to push him beyond his own capabilities outweigh the good that could come in achievement. That, however, should push us back to our original question, "Excellence for whose sake?"

True, if we push children out of selfish motives, we are wrong. As parents (or churches) we cannot afford to build our egos on their accomplishments. Likewise, if our example teaches that excellence is for personal advancement only, we have missed the point. But the only remaining option is not mediocrity! We must push toward excellence *for God's sake!*

Recently I was having breakfast with a young artist who had just accepted Christ a short time before. His testimony was exciting! For quite a number of years he had resisted giving his life to Christ because he was certain it would interfere with his work as an artist. For him art was everything. He worked as a staff artist with a large metropolitan newspaper, came home each day and took up his brushes to do free-lance work. There just didn't seem to be time to be both a good artist and a Christian. Finally, however, the emptiness of his life literally forced him to Christ. Then came the startling discovery: As a Christian he realized he was already becoming a better artist! He was able to concentrate better, to paint with greater feeling, and to actually paint more quickly. His growing excellence was in response to God. He literally was painting to the glory of God!

How different that encounter was from the one I had only a few months earlier with a man who, with some disgust, related an incident that took place in the church he attended. His wife had joined the choir at the church soon after they moved into the community. It was time for preparation for a seasonal cantata. There was only one word to describe that preparation—sloppy! Little or no extra effort was put into it. As time for the cantata drew near panic set in. But now it was too late to practice, so they prayed. After the concert the recurring comment from the choir members was, "Isn't it neat how the Holy Spirit pulled us through." How tragic! Do we really think God is honored when we do less than our best? Can we really believe that prayer is meant to bail us out of our mediocre preparation? Is this really a reflection of the glory of God?

I recently reread the account of the building of Solomon's Temple. I was impressed with the touch of excellence in all aspects of construction—the building materials, the workmen, the building plans, the dedication of the Temple, and the ensuing worship. It was done that way because Israel, at that point in her history, genuinely felt that God deserved the best. He still does!

Not much has been written about excellence from the perspective of God's glory. One recent exception to this is a book by Leroy Eims entitled *Be the Leader You Were Meant to Be.* In a chapter on excellence he relates the excellencies of God as the basis for our excellence. "God's name is excellent (Ps. 8:1) . . . God's lovingkindness is excellent (Ps. 36:7) . . . God's greatness is excellent (Ps. 150:1) . . . God's salvation is excellent (Isa. 12:2-5) . . . God's work is excellent (Deut. 32:1-4) . . . God's way is excellent (2 Sam. 22:31) . . . God's will is excellent (Rom. 12:1,2)."[4]

Excellence for whose sake? For God's sake, that's whose! Somehow in our homes and churches we must recapture the concept of doing all to the glory of God, for when we do we will certainly begin to insist on the best that each person can do.

What Do You Expect?

If excellence is to be a part of the climate for leadership, there will be the need to translate theory into expectation. Gardner again, in his book on the subject of excellence, says, "More and more we are coming to see that high performance, particularly where children are concerned, takes place in a framework of expectation. . . . If there are no expectations, there will be little high performance."[5]

Admittedly, we tread on dangerous ground here. Damage can be done by expecting more than can be produced as well as by expecting too little. But our tendency certainly leans toward "less" rather than "too much." Our children (and this also can apply to new Christians) must realize that we expect their best; further, those expectations must be apparent.

I spent a most interesting evening discussing some of the ideas contained in this book with a friend. We were pretty well taken up by our conversation and had not realized that his high-school-age son had been listening to us quite intently. As we talked about the matter of expectation and excellence, a most interesting twist in the conversation took place. The son broke into the conversation and said, "All I know is that I experienced a lot of pressure from friends at school to be mediocre. But the way my folks constantly encouraged me to do my best far outweighed that pressure." He went on to describe that parental encouragement as a foundation he would always look back to in the further development of his life!

That is precisely the point. We will not see excellent leaders moving into the world from our homes if we do not expect excellence in those homes.

It goes without saying, of course, that the expectation

of excellence must not only be verbalized, but also exemplified! Until parents expect excellence from themselves, it will be very hard to expect it from their children. William Glasser put it well in his book, *Reality Therapy:* "A parent who sits watching television, who never reads a book or demonstrates any of the values of using his intellect, will be hard pressed to teach the value of doing well in school through diligent study."[6]

This is all part of the overall climate for leadership which we focus on in this book. In our homes we must expect our best *for God's glory.* In our churches, also, we must have that commitment to excellence. Just because the church is an organization of primarily volunteer workers does not mean that we should expect inferior quality. Kenneth Gangel has bemoaned this tendency in his book, *Competent to Lead.* He says, "One of the great blights on the church in recent years has been its failure to establish strong and adequate systems of quality control. . . . The result has been the offering to God of shoddy workmanship and programming that does not pass the most elementary tests of adequacy."[7] If Gangel is correct (and I for one think he is), it is little wonder that we have difficulty producing effective leaders in our churches and homes. Without the expectation of excellence, there will be few who excel—it is as simple as that!

Perhaps nowhere in recent times is the matter of expectation and excellence better illustrated than in the story of Helen Keller. I recently reread that story and was impressed again at the fantastic accomplishment of this woman. But this was far from being a success story from the beginning. Helen was blind, deaf and dumb and was, frankly, a very poorly behaved girl. She was, after all, a handicapped child; at least that is how everyone excused her behavior. It was only when Annie Sullivan entered the picture that the story began to change. When she arrived in Alabama to be Helen's tutor and guardian she began the long process of development by demanding the best from her student. It involved a long and hard discipline, but through Annie Sullivan's high expectations Helen Keller reached her potential of excellence.

If, then, we are to create a climate for leadership development in our homes and churches, one of the basic ingredients must be a nourishment of all that is good and excellent. We can ill afford to be caught in the world's mold where just "getting by" is good enough. Rather, we must see that God calls us to our best as an act of worship to Him. Being better is not bad; it is good when we do it in the context of worship. We must encourage this attitude in every way possible. As parents and as church leaders we must expect excellence for the glory of God.

In the early '60s a young man began his college career at the University of Illinois. He was only an average student then. But early in his student experience Don was challenged by the idea of doing his best for God's glory. For him that became an immensely practical motive that meant discipline and hard work. From that time on a career unfolded that moved through a Ph.D. in mechanical engineering to a position at a leading Ivy League university. Today Don heads a significant research team in the area of biomechanics. I remember walking with him through a famous research facility where he was working during his sabbatical leave. Here I saw some of the orthopedic implants being used to repair anything from hip joints to fingers. I heard him tell of the improvements being made in this work—some of them as the result of a person dedicated to God and determined to be a leader marked by excellence. May it always be said of Christians that such excellence was never smothered but always nourished by our desire to glorify God!

Three

The Courage to Allow for Diversity

We say it in many different ways, but perhaps the most common expression is "variety is the spice of life." In scores of life-related instances we go on to prove the truth of that statement. When sitting down to eat we hope for at least some selection of food from which to choose. And we really do not want the same meal for dinner each evening of the week. For many women the sight of someone else wearing a similar dress is depressing. We want to be different. Men love to be able to tell a joke no one else has heard; variety adds life to the party, after all! Car makers know that to be successful in their business they must give their customers a choice of models. We watch our daily routine turn into boredom until we finally plan different activities from time to time to pick ourselves up.

The blessing of variety can be seen in the opening pages of the Bible. One phrase repeated several times in the first chapter of Genesis is God's verdict on His creation: "It is good!" In each case that statement follows the creation of something different. It was the diversity of creation that made it so beautiful and good. That truth can be confirmed whether studying snowflakes or planets, insects or people's faces. Diversity is built right into the fabric of life as God made it.

Of all people it would seem that Christians should not resist this natural tendency toward diversity in life. In our churches we should welcome all kinds of people. In our homes we should be open to a variety of vocational possibilities. Unfortunately, however, that is not always the case. A great many people expect and require "sameness" in life. However, when the climate in our homes and churches becomes too restrictive, one of the ingredients that goes into the development of leadership is cut off.

I recall vividly the reaction of many of my friends to a church built near us several years ago. This was a solid, Bible-believing church that was respected in the community. They dared to experiment! And they dared to do it before it became popular. To start with, instead of the traditional rectangular shape, their building was round. In place of traditional pews, there were individual plastic seats. The roof line swept up to a high center focal point. At that time, many Christian people simply were not ready for this kind of departure from tradition. But to a watching world it had a tremendously positive testimony. As a result, the church grew as it reached out to others in leadership.

What does all of this have to do with developing new leaders? As we seek to influence people toward leadership, it will be imperative that we commit ourselves to allow for diversity in our homes and churches—diversity in styles, interests, work, economic status, music, etc. For out of that exciting climate of diversity leaders can emerge in many different fields without the fetter of having to fit into a predetermined mold. And these will be leaders with hearts and minds open to all kinds of people and possibilities!

Equality Is Not Similarity

"But," someone remonstrates, "isn't the genius of Christianity in the fact that we are all equal?" Certainly one cannot argue with that statement—unless, of course, we are fuzzy about the meaning of equality. Whenever we see the idea of equality presented in Scripture, it carries the idea of equal standing before God, equal opportunity to be God's child, equal worth in God's family. It is false, however, to move from equality to similarity.

Even a little thinking at this point will help us understand this truth. I recently made a dreaded trip. It was not to the doctor's office, hospital, or mortuary. It was to the women's clothing section of a large department store to buy my wife a birthday gift. I happen to feel very uncomfortable buying ladies' clothing! But I bravely waded into the section where robes were sold. What I discovered was more equality than I had counted on. The prices for the various robes were very close to each other; quality appeared to be equal. I assure you, though, that the robes were not at all similar! Which color, what length, zip up or button, fuzzy or plain—all these choices faced me. The clerk assured me that I could not go wrong with any of the robes because they were of equal value. That was little comfort as I worked my way through the diverse collection.

I recently visited a new and unique restaurant. Much to my surprise, every lunch on the menu was almost exactly the same price. It could be said that they were of virtually equal value. Even though I am not a nutritional expert, I suspect there was little difference nutritionally in the various lunches (one being as bad as another). But in taking a quick glance at other tables to see what other people had ordered, I can assure you that the lunches were not similar to each other! Variety was what had made this a popular spot at which to eat.

There is no better illustration of this truth to be found in Scripture than the one given by the apostle Paul in 1 Corinthians 12. His simple but profound use of the human body pictures for us the beautiful lesson of diversity. Of course each part of the body has equal value. In fact, Paul says we give honor to the less conspicuous parts to equalize the honor (is that why ladies wear earrings?). Equality certainly does not mean similarity, though. It is the variety of functions that makes the body work efficiently. Can you imagine the whole body being one giant eyeball rolling down the street? Paul could not! For the body to be what it should be, each individual and diverse part must be allowed to develop. Then the whole body will be developed and strengthened.

I wonder how many of our homes and churches resemble Paul's ludicrous giant eyeball. Could it be that we have stifled people's creative ability to develop as leaders by trying to press them into the mold of "sameness"?

What a joy it is to meet someone like the father who recently was in my office to talk about how things were going in his home. "We have finally caught on to something very important," he confessed. "Our one daughter is simply not an academic-type person. We have been trying to make her a scholar like her sister, and it just isn't working. So we have decided to encourage her in her home economics courses where she really shines." Because of that wise parental attitude, there is a girl who has a great chance to develop her potential in a field completely different from her sister.

Unfortunately, many homes and even more churches are characterized by a climate quite different from the one in the home just described. Much too often, similarity is seen as a distinct plus. The people we honor are the ones who "fit in" the best. That very similarity, though, deadens the possible development of effective leadership. New ideas are treated with suspicion. People who are different from the rest of the group are never quite allowed into the real circle of friendship. And, disappointingly, new leaders never seem to emerge on the scene.

What a special privilege it is, on the other hand, to be a part of a Christian community that truly practices equality without similarity—where I can feel comfortable and important no matter what my gifts and abilities are. What an even greater privilege it is to be a member of a family that practices equality without insisting on similarity—where I can honestly be encouraged to develop my life as God gave it to me!

Do Differences Breed Divisions?

It is not merely coincidental that Scripture passages speaking of diversity also stress unity. Going back to the twelfth chapter of 1 Corinthians we see an excellent illustration of this. Early in the chapter Paul makes a special point of showing that the diversity of gifts in the church has a basic unity in origin. All of them come from the triune Godhead. Later in the chapter that unity is then applied to the church when we are reminded that gifts must be used for the *profit of all.* It is the unity and health of the whole body that is important.

This sort of discussion in Scripture reminds us of two very important facts: First, diversity can lead to division; second, diversity can actually strengthen unity! In our fear of the first truth we may miss the second. For the cause of leadership development that would be a shame.

Of course, there is no point in burying our heads in the sand regarding the fact that diversity can breed division. It has happened often enough to put legitimate fear in the hearts of some. If you doubt this, just think for a moment about what often happens to the boy in the youth group who does not like sports, or the new couple in the young adult class who have decided that they would like to have six children, or the church board member who wonders aloud why we have to have revival meetings again this year when no one came last year, or the young lady who decides she would like to pursue a career in ballet even though her parents have never seen one. Being different certainly carries with it the seeds of exclusion and division.

On at least two occasions in my ministry I have had people honestly express fears to me about "new people attending our church" because it would upset the family atmosphere where everyone thought alike. Whole denominations have sheltered themselves from the influence of others since new ideas might break up the "spirit of unity."

What a happy contrast to find a group of Christians who thrive in their diversity. Recently our church hired a new director of Christian education. I still wonder what his thoughts were as he sat in on his first church board meeting. A proposal was being made for the purchase of a rather expensive piece of equipment. With the diversity of opinions and interests represented on that board, there came a definite diversity of ideas regarding the merits of the purchase! After a spirited debate, a vote was taken and the equipment purchase was approved by a majority vote. Did that disagreement mean division? Not at all! When the meeting concluded, quite a number of the board members still went out to eat together. They were very much friends despite the diverse opinions. And that very diversity had sharpened everyone's thinking in the process of the discussion.

This is the positive side of the coin. Diversity brings strength! There is nothing quite as deadening as a group that is so alike they never disagree. The apostles of Christ were certainly not a group like that. This collection of tax collectors, fishermen, and political zealots was unique because its unity came from its diversity, not in place of it. In the early church that same blend of various temperaments brought strength. Peter and Paul could disagree over eating companions, but ultimately truth would emerge as such confrontation forced people to think through the issue. Paul and Barnabas could disagree over the choice of traveling companions, but ultimately the missionary force doubled and they went about doing God's work.

What we cannot afford to do is kill the initiative of someone whose only sin is to have interests different from ours. If we do we will have smothered the very spark that could flame into leadership.

I have followed with interest the development of a young man we will call Bill. Without a doubt there is a fairly long line of people who have willingly predicted failure for Bill. It seemed that wherever he was, he was disruptive. The school for missionaries' children which he attended finally asked that he be removed from school. He was definitely possessed of different ideas and was not fitting in. The Bible college he attended was not sure what to do with him. His grades were good, but again he defied the mold. And he made the mistake of assuming that among Christian friends he could share his ideas. He finally left the college; he just did not fit in. His first attempt at Christian service met with the same rebuff. In that particular organization new ideas were not welcome. You were paid to "do," not to "think." He left because he did not fit in. Finally, and fortunately, there was an organization ready to welcome a young man who dared to think creative thoughts. Here diversity was seen as a strength and all the pent-up potential in Bill was released. Today Bill plays a key role in a large Christian organization—one which realizes that differences do not need to breed divisions.

Do All to the Glory of God

One of the factors limiting openness to diversity is the lingering confusion which still exists in some people's minds as to what the "Lord's work" really is. When that tag is given as a limitation it really clouds the possibility of healthy diversity. While many people seem to have conquered the old "secular/sacred" dichotomy in their minds, it is harder to accept at a feeling level.

The problem is not helped, of course, when a well-meaning missionary suggests that before you accept second best for your child you should pray that God will call him into Christian service. It is also not helped by the super-spiritual businessman who proclaims for all to hear that he only works to earn enough to live; his real work is witnessing for the Lord! More than likely, both of these people speak honestly. But they fail to realize the havoc they might be playing in someone else's life as they struggle with vocational choices.

I was discussing this very subject with members of a Sunday School class one day when one of the class members made a most interesting confession. "I struggled for many years with this problem," he said. "As a boy I was constantly told that the highest goal I could strive for was to be a pastor or a missionary. When I felt no inclination to either, I also felt little motivation to excel in any other work." He went on to recount his struggle with guilt feelings over his right to be successful at anything since he did not choose to be a pastor or missionary.

I suspect that story could be repeated many times. How many young people are interested in writing—but not necessarily "Christian" novels where everyone gets converted and lives happily ever after, music—but not gospel, journalism—but not for the denominational magazine, teaching—but not necessarily in a Christian school? Many either squelch their interest or are lost to the Christian cause altogether. Don't misunderstand. There is nothing wrong with Christian novels, gospel music, denominational magazines, or Christian schools. But there is also nothing wrong with good literature, classical music, the local newspaper, or public schools per se! We must allow people the freedom to excel in any legitimate endeavor of life. It is out of such diversity that widespread influence for God can result.

Paul said in 1 Corinthians 10:31 that we are to "do *all* to the glory of God." The glory of God is the standard for excellence in our work (as we have already discussed in chapter 2), while the "all" is the invitation to diversity. It should be noted in passing that if people are concerned that this emphasis on diversity will diminish the population of the so-called "full-time Christian ministry," their fears are unfounded. I cannot help but believe that if we really encouraged people to do whatever they did to God's glory, the influence for God would be greater than ever. And out of that context we would see a flow of people into church-related ministries as well. Commitment to God's will and glory is, after all, a seedbed for use in God's kingdom, wherever that may be.

How do we foster the spirit of diversity? Are there practical ways to really convince ourselves and others that *all* can be done to the glory of God? Certainly there must be.

Perhaps a church should sponsor a "vocational conference" with the same vigor as a "missionary conference." What would happen if a weekend was devoted to messages on the legitimacy of diverse vocational possibilities, seminars on necessary preparation for various professions, panels featuring outstanding Christian leaders in a variety of fields, and display booths illustrating that variety? Chances are it would be a healthy experience not only for those seeking information but also for those providing it! Certainly every church should at least keep a current set of catalogs from a wide variety of Christian colleges and universities for young people and their parents to look at.

It seems that sensitive parents could do something very similar in their own homes. As children move from daydreaming to serious thinking about "what they will be when they grow up," part of the family devotional period could be devoted to a study of some of those areas of interest. What does it take to prepare to become a fireman or doctor or a good mother? What challenges does a Christian face as a lawyer or executive secretary or soldier? Any good public library can start a child off in his discovery. Very possibly there are people in the local Christian community who could add expertise. A visit to some people in the various occupations might not be the worst idea. Local colleges could undoubtedly offer advice regarding preparation requirements.

The point of all this, of course, is to encourage children to think widely as they search for God's will for their lives. We want them to think as widely as the gifts and abilities God can give! And with that broad look we want them to realize that whatever they do, as long as it is in God's will and for God's glory, can be done with excellence. With that sort of "choice-freedom" there is no reason why we can't see leaders who are Christians affecting a great diversity of occupations and professions. Truly we can do *all* to the glory of God!

Encourage, Don't Push

The entire principle of diversity has an opposite side of the coin which should be considered. Here and there we will run into people (less seldom, churches) who allow the pendulum to swing to an opposite extreme. These are people who pride themselves on being "nontraditional" in virtually everything. In an effort to prove this freedom from previously accepted patterns, they push themselves and their children into molds that are artificially contrived. What results is not genuine diversity but more probably nothing other than selfish pride.

Janet spoke to me one day with genuine concern about her husband. "Bob really scares me. Over the last few months he has bought almost a whole new wardrobe so he can present a new image." I had noticed the very same thing in Bob. Janet went on to explain that Bob was now considering a shift of careers to enter a field that, while not necessarily wrong, was certainly out of the ordinary among Christians.

Janet's second concern was the negative influence all this was having on their young son. It seemed he was unconsciously mimicking his father. He too had taken on habits and dress options which were "far out" as he described it. His circle of friends had changed and his actions were causing trouble at school.

While conversing with Bob I started to uncover the problem. Rather than being happy with what he was, he was out to "prove that a Christian doesn't have to be boxed into the traditional patterns." And he was going to see that his son also avoided this dreaded trap. This was one of those times, however, when the cure was worse than the disease!

How much better it would have been if that attitude of openness to diversity could have been used to simply *encourage* a life direction rather than *force* one. By contrast I recall two brothers who had sons of approximately the same age. While both brothers were very artistic, it became evident that only one of the sons would follow that pattern. The other brother's son was a sports nut! It took a great deal of grace for that boy's father to watch his son play football instead of play in an orchestra. But he did! And he encouraged his son to become a good football player. He was a father with the sense to encourage an obvious ability in his son rather than push him into artistic endeavor for which he had little or no aptitude.

When we learn not to be afraid of diversity we will take a giant step forward in creating the climate for leadership development. A spirit will then be developed in our homes and Christian institutions that will allow genuine respect for people with a variety of interests, abilities, and vocations. Together we can encourage one another to develop our lives in the unique pattern God has for us. We need not feel threatened by those who are different from us; rather, we can thank God for the infinite variety He has put within His family.

Yes, this will take courage. It is much more comfortable to have people be like us. But if we are genuinely interested in developing leaders who will make an impact for God and good in our world, we will need to exercise that courage. "Sameness" never encourages creative leadership; the God-blessed pattern of diversity among people can, however. We have the task of genuinely welcoming diversity in our homes and churches, for that is part of the climate for leadership.

Four

Living with a Single Eye

Although fans of the popular television series "Little House on the Prairie" would find it hard to believe, Michael Landon, who plays the head of the Ingalls family, describes himself in early years as a boy who was a "scared, self-conscious little squirt." The *Chicago Tribune* article which told this story (April 6, 1977) went on to describe a most interesting fact about Landon. While in a ninth-grade gym class, Michael tossed a javelin 80 feet. "The gym teacher got all excited. He told me I had the potential to become a top javelin thrower if I worked at it. I took the javelin home and threw it every day for hours and hours," he said. He went on to make the track team in high school and had 45 scholarship offers from colleges as a result of his ability. Landon concluded, "Everybody has something marvelous he can do. He just needs encouragement and direction. Once a kid gets that, it can change his whole life." Even though Landon changed his life direction, this experience served as a foundation.

The point is well taken! The lives of all effective leaders are characterized by a real sense of direction. It could be described as life lived with a "single eye." Time is not wasted on peripheral issues, nor is it lost by worrying about what cannot be done. Rather, it learns to zero in on what can be done, and then does it well!

Leaders I have had the privilege of meeting have had this clear mark of focus in their lives. Pastors, broadcasters, politicians, musicians, salespersons—they all had a very clear understanding of their task and their ability to perform that task. And with a singleness of purpose they set about to accomplish their goal in life.

Knowing this, it should be apparent that here is a truth that must become a part of the climate for leadership. We must understand the concept of "living with a single eye" as well as know how to communicate it to those in our homes and churches.

A Circle with One Center

Periodically (which means "not as often as I should") I go to our church gymnasium to work out for a while. Inevitably, I end up getting a basketball and shooting some baskets before I am done. Just as inevitably, and despite my determination that it will not happen, I pick out the one basketball that is not properly balanced. For some unknown reason, I seem drawn to that ball.

There are many people, unfortunately, who are like that basketball. Their lives are missing the target because they are not properly balanced. They lack that clear integration point around which everything else can revolve. They are not clear about what they can or should be doing. As a result they do nothing well and they are frustrated over it.

This is illustrated vividly in the lives of two brothers I know. The end of the story, which in this case needs to be told first, is that one brother has dropped out of school, served time in prison, and bounced from one job to another. He has lost touch with his family and, in the process, has aligned himself with a circle of friends who are basically drifters. The other brother graduated from high school, is attending college, and has settled into a productive life.

The irony of this story is that the first brother was probably more talented than the second. He gave evidence of great communicative skills. But no one ever managed to challenge him to develop those skills. He never really became interested in anything. By contrast, the second brother was interested in music. Frankly, he was not that good, but he worked hard at it. As his skills increased, his opportunity to broaden his experiences also increased. Music became a central point in his life, and it still is. From that center point came the well-rounded development evident in him today.

There are those who feel that a child's development can actually be traced by following the progressively developing center point of his life. A child has a unique organizing ability which can and should be encouraged. He can actively put his world together from some central point of interest.

When that center point is missing, or when it is confused and unclear, all of life becomes confused with it. The rationale for development is gone because there is no meaningful goal. The apostle James describes such a person as "double-minded" and "unstable" (see Jas. 1:8). Leadership potential simply cannot be developed if there is a lack of some clearly-defined center point in a person's life.

It goes without saying that in the course of a child's life that center point will change. Any child with a fair sense of imagination will discover different points of interest which become the basis for his activity at a given time. For a while a boy may be a detective. He will read detective stories and dream of solving the world's most baffling crime. His sister, meanwhile, may take a great interest in gymnastics. This will become a focus for her attention. Those focus points in each of them may very well change from time to time, but if they are encouraged it is likely that eventually something will settle in as *the* lasting center point. Then a young person will develop a direction for a lifetime.

I have had educator friends of mine tell me that the greatest gift any parent can give a child is the encouragement of an active imagination. I am sure that is true. From imagination, activity can be organized—as a leader organizes his life around his dreams and goals.

It is perhaps in this area more than any other that television has had such a devastating effect. When a child (or adult, for that matter) spends huge amounts of time merely observing the results of someone else's imaginative work, his own mind is dulled. That only creates a vicious cycle where the inactive mind becomes less imaginative, and thus even more inactive. Time that could have been used in the exciting development of a life with focus is, instead, frittered away on a potpourri of widely varying and usually worthless entertainment.

We honestly owe it to our children to encourage them to discover a center point for their lives. We owe it to our fellow Christians to exhibit a life based on one goal and direction. No other option is open to us if we are to see the development of effective leaders.

The Way HE Should Go!

Is this concept merely the observation of educators and psychologists, or does it have some basis in Scripture? A most interesting answer to that question came to my attention just recently.

One evening a friend mentioned to me that he had heard a message on Proverbs 22:6 ("Train up a child in the way he should go; and when he is old, he will not depart from it") in which the entire emphasis was on the word "he." Since this contradicted the usual interpretation I had heard for this verse, I knew I would have to check it out more carefully.

For years I had heard this verse explained with an emphasis on the word "way." If you were faithful in showing a child the proper way to go in life, you could rest in the fact that eventually that child would follow the right way. I have heard testimonies from parents who have seen this happen with their own children. Following a period of backsliding, the child returned to the Lord and His way for his life.

If, of course, the emphasis in this verse is on the word "he," it changes things considerably. After consulting some of the best Old Testament commentaries, I discovered that indeed the word "he" is the point of emphasis. That means that the thrust of this verse is to encourage parents to assist their children in pursuing that direction in life for which they are particularly suited. The verse, then, really says more about vocational choices than it does spiritual choices. Granted, it assumes a spiritual base in which we want God's will, but it then builds on that base by insisting that a focus on God's direction is imperative to a meaningful life.

For the first few years I knew Harold he was little more than a prank-prone playboy. At church he impressed everyone with his happy-go-lucky attitude toward life. Many people were concerned that Harold simply was not growing up as he should; he lacked any clear sense of direction in his life, either spiritually or vocationally.

Harold's family and friends were encouraged when he decided to attend a Christian college. Maybe this was a signal that he was finally going to settle down and get serious about life in general and his life in particular. But such was not the case. He only managed to be a fly in the ointment at college, just as he had been in everything else.

That probably would have been the end of the story, except for one very wise and sensitive professor. In a history class this professor noted that Harold showed unusual interest. He was not learning facts by memory merely to pass exams; he was genuinely interacting with the material. The professor suggested some additional projects that would challenge Harold's interest, and Harold accepted the challenge with enthusiasm.

With that class began an adventure that has now led this young man into advanced academic degrees and a promising future in the field of history. As he focused his attention on the way *he* should go, he was able to put every part of his life together meaningfully. His spiritual life also showed dramatic growth. He exhibited powers of concentration that many thought would be impossible for him—all because one professor was wise enough to sense a direction in Harold's life and help him train in the way he should go.

When psychologists tell us that each child in a family should be encouraged to pursue some positive goal independent of those taken by other children in the family, they are simply repeating this proverb! We start by accepting the God-given principle of diversity (as discussed in chapter 3) and then move on to encourage a definite focus on that goal which is the unique property of each individual.

Focus Gives Direction

Without some clear focal point in life we are really without clear direction or aim. On the other hand, if there is a clear center point in the circle of our lives there can also be a definite sense of purpose and direction. James L. Cooper said it well: "Most people fail not because they are bad, not because they don't have resources, not because the circumstances of life hem them in; they fail because they do not live decisively."[8] We might add that they do not live decisively because they do not have any goal clearly in focus; they have no feel for what they should be doing.

One of the clearest lessons regarding the relationship between focus and a sense of direction in life comes from the Old Testament character Nehemiah. If there is any one key that unlocks the secret to Nehemiah's success, it is his clear understanding of what he was to do with his life. He may have been only a king's servant at one time, but the factor that led him to great accomplishment was his clear sense of commitment to lead Israel to a renewal of national life.

When Nehemiah returned to Jerusalem he was faced with staggering odds against him. For as much as 90-100 years Jews had now been living in Jerusalem, following their exile. But the walls were still not rebuilt. People were depressed and discouraged, and national pride simply did not exist. However, Nehemiah focused on what had to be done and was determined that his focus would dictate the direction of his energies.

When the Jews caught Nehemiah's vision and began to work with that same focus, things began to happen. Walls were being built! Pride was returning! But vocal opposition from surrounding regions was also developing. Again, though, Nehemiah would not be deterred from the goal set before him. He continued to focus on his task. It is interesting to note the way Nehemiah responded to an invitation from his enemies to hold peace talks. "I am doing a great work and I cannot come down!" (see Neh. 6:3). Here was a life marked by focus-producing direction.

Nehemiah's example is certainly no different from the experience of leaders in our world today. Leaders are people with a clear sense of direction. They have focused on a goal and are working to achieve it.

If we are to see leaders emerging from our homes and churches, we must also encourage "life with a single eye." That is what will motivate people, under God's direction, to the hard work which can equip them for leadership.

It would be naive to suggest that early in life a child must know what he is going to do for the rest of his life. His focus will need to be much more short-range in the early years. It is perfectly legitimate, though, to strongly encourage those short-range goals so as to develop a pattern of goal-setting that will lead to clear-cut, long-range goals in due time.

In every child's life there are ample opportunities for short-range goals. The first summer our son wanted to play in Little League baseball, I was not sure he could do it. When we would play catch together in the yard he would duck away from the ball as often as he would try to catch it. I could not imagine what he would do with a "hot grounder" in a real game. But it was obvious that he had his heart set on playing. So we focused our attention for several weeks, preparing for the season. We went to our church gym, even though it was still winter, and practiced catching grounders, pop flies, and line drives. Doug worked hard because he was living with a single eye toward Little League competition. When formal practices started he continued to work night after night. Imagine the thrill he experienced on the night he received the first game ball for outstanding play at shortstop. And we were all thrilled when he was named to one of the All-Star teams at the end of the season! None of that would have happened had he not focused clearly on his goal.

Whether it be Little League baseball, school projects,

piano lessons, Bible memorization, or book reading we have a responsibility to help children set their minds on achieving goals. For from that climate of working toward goals will come the ultimate ability to see larger goals formulated. Finally a life goal can come into focus for which they will work with determination. Life suddenly will take on a definite direction. Children will have grown into adults who know what they want to accomplish in life. And you can be sure that from that group will emerge leaders for God's glory!

Don't Miss the Obvious

For the Christian a discussion about focus in life has an obvious beginning point. We are called to put God at the center of our lives. The promise is that as God and His will become the focus of living, all other pieces in life's puzzle will begin to fall into place as well. Putting God first is not an option in opposition to clear vocational goals, though. It is, rather, the necessary corollary. When God is the center of our focus He can then lead us to vocational goals consistent with His will. In that way our life goals will be superimposed over the major goal of serving God.

The obvious advantage this gives the Christian is that he gets God's help in establishing his life goals. That is why Scripture consistently encourages us to make certain God has the central place in our lives.

There are many passages that speak directly to this issue. While the scope of this book does not allow a complete commentary on such passages, we ought to at least take a cursory glance at some of them. If nothing else, it will remind us that God desires that we have the right focus in life.

Matthew 5:8: "Blessed are the pure in heart: for they shall see God." The point of this verse from the Beatitudes has often been missed. When Jesus says that the pure in heart shall be happy (blessed), He is not speaking primarily of moral correctness. Rather, the words indicate a single purpose of heart. He is indicating that a person whose purpose of heart is unmixed with any competing goals (thus is "pure"), whose attention is focused clearly on God—that person will *see God!* He will discover what he is looking for as long as he looks with focus.

Matthew 6:33: "But seek ye first the kingdom of God, and his righteousness; and all these things shall be added unto you." Later in the Sermon on the Mount Jesus gave one of the better-known commands regarding focus. This verse illustrates the point made earlier about proper focus helping all other parts of our lives fit together. If we will set our priority goal on the right object (seek first God's kingdom and righteousness), all other matters of concern will fall in place and life will fit together as it should (all other things will be yours as well).

1 Corinthians 9:24-26: "Know ye not that they which run in a race run all, but one receiveth the prize? So run, that ye may obtain. And every man that striveth for the mastery is temperate in all things. Now they do it to obtain a corruptible crown; but we an incorruptible. I therefore so run, not as uncertainly; so fight I, not as one that beateth the air." Paul, in characteristically vivid language, illustrates the principle of focus in these verses. A runner does not win a race if he does not have victory as a clear-cut goal. The self-control needed to train and compete comes only when the focus is clear. Likewise, Paul says, he will also exercise self-control in his life because he has a clearly defined goal of being accepted by God. If he is to reach that goal he cannot afford to be sidetracked by issues that are peripheral to it.

Hebrews 11. This entire chapter is a review of the principle of focus. The author cites person after person as having succeeded because he had his eye on God and by faith was not deterred from that single purpose. Some were tempted to other goals by their success while others were tempted by severe persecution. But every one stayed true to God because he was clear in his goal!

James 1:8: "A double minded man is unstable in all his ways." In this verse James gives us the negative side of the coin. It is the double-minded man who is unstable. He wants to please God on one hand, but he also wants to set his eye on other goals and place them in the priority position reserved for God. In that confusion he is a loser, for James tells us that he will not receive anything from the Lord! Therefore, while the double-minded man thinks he can get the best of two worlds he actually gets neither, because he fails to live with a single eye.

What all these passages are saying to us is that if we are weak in producing leaders, a major part of the problem may be that our homes and churches do not encourage a high level of commitment. If it is true that even good vocational decisions grow out of proper focus on God (and I firmly believe that is true), then the real cure for vocational confusion will be a renewal of that first attention to God.

In a society that presses in on us with so many demands we must call forth our best to really put God at the center of our lives. We need to resist the temptation to kid ourselves about our commitment through the use of "God talk." We have to learn to take a very realistic look at ourselves—what is really first in our lives? For what do we spend most of our time and energy? Francis Schaeffer, in a sermon entitled "Ash Heap Lives," talks about the danger of Christians becoming guilty of practical materialism where "we spend most of our time and money for things that will end up in the city dump."[9] If we are caught in that trap we are certainly candidates for the "double-minded" award.

The whole discussion about focus in life is terribly important because it is at the heart of our value system. How we are living betrays what is at the center of our lives. I have looked with great respect at the life of a business-man friend of our family. He entered a large company in an upper-level management position. That position was producing a comfortable income for his family. Within just a few years, however, the young president of the firm suddenly resigned and Walt was asked to take over leadership of the company. This meant a substantial increase in both salary and prestige. But Walt was determined that if he took the job he would still maintain his commitment to put God first. He stoutly resisted the temptation to move up the ladder in terms of home, car, clothing, etc., because he was afraid of clouding his focus on God. For him God had to stay in the center of his life whether he was company president or not. And he has continued to prove that "God first" can be compatible with excellent leadership in his new position.

If it is really true, as some suggest, that as few as five percent of all people have a definite aim for their lives, it is little wonder that the leadership field always has openings. Of all people, Christians should be prepared to fill that void. They can, to the degree they learn and practice the art of "living with a single eye."

Five

Passing on the Formula, Not the Product

Public school administrators have exposure to a more significant cross section of families than most of us. A good friend who is superintendent of a large public school district was sharing with me some of his thoughts about leadership when he made a profound statement: "Don, the problem so often is that parents are more concerned with passing on the product of their work than the formula for achieving the product." How true!

Undoubtedly our motives are right when we seek to pass on to our children a comfortable life-style free of trouble, but the results can be so tragic when it comes to developing leaders. All of us have heard at one time or another the typical story of "cute little Sammy" who grew up in a home where nothing was too good for him. Little Sammy may have been treated to exclusive camps, boarding schools, a fine car at graduation, and a secure position in father's firm after college. But, as so often happens, fortunes change quickly. And little Sammy ends up being a person who cannot hold a job, whose marriage is shaky, and whose life is falling apart. The problem is that little Sam had been dominated by a protective father and was completely unprepared to face life as it is. What was meant by his father as a great gift (the product of his years of work) turned out to be robbery of the most important gift (the formula for work and achievement learned through personal experience).

It is always easier, of course, to see the ghost of over-protection in someone else than in ourselves. How do we work with our own children—that is the crucial question. Do we simply take hands off? Is it so wrong to want to spare our children difficulty?

Each Man for Himself

If we are to successfully offer the formula rather than the product to our children, there is a basic attitude that must characterize us: *Whatever responsibility we may have toward others never goes so far as to destroy that individual's own personal responsibility.* We are stewards, not owners. And that applies to parents' attitudes to children, pastors' attitudes to parishioners, and friends' attitudes to each other. Ultimately before God it is still "each man for himself."

It may be that the flood of self-help books for parents in recent years has hurt our understanding of this principle. After a while parents may feel that everything is up to them. We trace every problem in an adult to a mistake his parents made when he was a child. Don't get me wrong— our influence on children is enormous! But it never takes away from the ultimate responsibility of the individual.

If I understand this basic concept I can allow my children the privilege of learning life's lessons without constant interference. My worth as a parent is not always at stake. I no longer have to hover over my child to keep him from all errors just so others will think well of me.

It is this basic tenet of personal responsibility that should characterize the climate of our Christian homes and institutions. In our heritage there have been people who died for the truth of "the priesthood of the believer." If we understand anything at all about Scripture it is that God deals with each of us as individuals—we are created with personal responsibility and we will be judged personally. This concept, you see, affects the training of our children. It is no longer sufficient to force a Christian life-style on them; rather we must lead them to discover for themselves the truth that changes lives. It even goes farther than this. Danger, disappointment, failure, frustration—all must eventually be learned personally through experience. We rob our children of an important ingredient of leadership development if we deny them the privilege of learning even the negative parts of life through personal experience.

John was a middle-aged man who came to see me in great distress over his daughter. Now in her mid-twenties, she had always been a source of almost constant grief to her family. She lived with a succession of men, moved from petty shoplifting to more serious crime, rejected all the social values of her parents, and defied God in her life. As I talked with her father I saw only one consistent factor emerge—his willingness to bail her out of all situations!

John was convinced that if he could just once get his daughter to do things his way all trouble would end. When I suggested that benign (but loving) neglect might be the best therapy she could receive, he was taken aback. It was almost impossible for him to accept the fact that sooner or later he had to let her live her own life and be personally responsible for the consequences of her actions. How much better if he had helped her learn that lesson through guided experience 20 years sooner!

Jay Kesler, president of Youth for Christ International, put it well in his book, *Let's Succeed with Our Teenagers.* He talks about the rights our children have to succeed or fail, to choose wisely or unwisely, to please God or disobey Him. But, as he points out, this is hard to accept. "We would like to influence him [our child] to choose only right and good. If we do this, however, we find ourselves doing the very thing that God Himself refuses to do."[10] There is the key! We have to begin from God's vantage point, *every man for himself!*

But What About the Risks?

Of course there are risks when we determine not to be overprotective. It would be foolish to think otherwise. The risks run from somewhat innocuous matters (will that 50¢ allowance be spent wisely?) to the most serious issues of life (will the choice be to serve God or not?). Those widely differing risks are related, however. If we will allow a child to learn the consequences of a misspent allowance when he is young, we can teach an important lesson regarding choices and consequences that could prevent bad decisions on greater issues later.

The theory of natural consequences in discipline has gained popularity in recent years. Put simply, it is the willingness to let a child experience the relationship between his action and the consequence of that action. Late to supper?—go hungry tonight! Put off homework?—get a lower grade!

There isn't a good leader alive who does not face hard decisions, all of which carry important consequences. Many times those consequences will reach into other people's lives. With each decision is also a risk, but the decision must be made. To put it off is really a decision—and not a very good one most of the time. How can we hope to develop leaders with decision-making ability if we refuse to let that ability develop because of our overprotection?

Bruce Narramore in his book *Help! I'm a Parent* speaks of the relationship between this overprotection and poor personal development: "Instead of letting children assume responsibility for their own actions, we are tempted to intervene to 'protect' them. . . . Every time this happens we deprive children of their responsibility by sheltering them from natural consequences. This promotes an unhealthy dependency on parents and stifles emotional maturity."[11]

I am sure it must have taken a great deal of courage for David's parents to let him continue tending the sheep after he had been attacked by wild animals. Talk about risk! How many of us would let our children tangle with bears and lions. But that was an essential part of David's preparation for leadership. He learned that God could keep him in dangerous situations. There came a day when that lesson gave him courage to take on the giant, Goliath. Armed with the formula for courage which he had been privileged to learn, he could lead Israel to victory.

This willingness to accept the risk associated with letting children make decisions is probably harder for Christian parents than for others. We are more aware of the eternal dangers involved. There is a legitimate concern for the spiritual ramifications of decision making. But that is still no reason to step in and protect our children from those risks. What we can do, however, is *guide* them in decision making! Perhaps there is no better way to do this than through the example of our own decision making!

I am sure that most of my ideas about money were learned by observation. Growing up in a pastor's home gave me many chances to see how consequences follow decisions in the area of finances. Because my parents made good decisions they were able to raise four children, see them all graduate from college, retire with a home debt free—and all on a limited income. Though I started working part-time when I was in the seventh grade, I can never remember my father telling me how to spend money (with the exception of *strong* encouragement to tithe!). I know I made some foolish decisions with that money, but I was allowed to live with the consequences of my own decisions. It was the combination of those consequences, along with the example of wise decisions by my parents, that formed my own attitudes toward money.

Risks? Yes, there are risks to take if we are to allow children to experience the consequences of their actions. But it is the freedom to learn from those decisions that is part of the bridge to leadership. We dare not deny our children the privilege of crossing that bridge on their own.

The Hardest Job

We still have not talked about the hardest job for parents—to keep from living their lives through the lives of their children. If we are serious about developing leaders, this is a trait we will have to deal with honestly and firmly.

We cannot afford to rationalize true reasons for developing dependency in our children. If that dependency is more for our emotional needs as parents than for the development of the child, we not only hurt ourselves but we blunt the possibility of our children becoming strong, independent leaders.

A young mother came to my office one day to share her frustration about her first-grade daughter. Morning after morning she had to nag at her daughter to get her up, virtually dress her herself, and gather all her belongings together so she would not be late for school. After some discussion with her I became aware that the mother was not nearly so concerned about the welfare of the daughter as she was about her own pride, "It seems like I would be a bad mother if my girl was late for school!" Eventually she came to realize that the best way to solve the problem was to stop nagging and let the girl be late for school. One tardy mark did wonders to get the girl up and moving again.

I can recall so vividly one evening after our first child was born when, with company present, our daughter decided to cry loud and long at bedtime. It was very tempting to let her stay up rather than cry because we felt like bad parents just then—especially in front of our guests. But she needed her rest more than we needed our egos boosted, so she cried and soon slept.

Any mother of a teenage daughter goes through times when choice of clothing becomes a point of conflict. Too many times we want children to dress our way not because it is better or safer, but because we want others to think well of us as parents. We, in effect, live our lives through our children. It might be good to examine our motives when we seek to impose our will on our children. Is it really to "help them" or is it an attempt to "help ourselves" through them?

It is worth noting that Christian institutions can fall into this same trap; and it has the same negative effect on the climate for leadership development. I recall one friend telling of the problem he encountered with a Christian school his children attended. A list of books had been prepared which could *not* be read by the students. However, there were some books on that list that the friend honestly felt his children should read if they were to have a well-rounded education. As it turned out, it appeared the list had been prepared not so much to spare the children as to impress the constituency of the school. Like some parents, the school was living its life through its students.

It might have been much easier for the father of the prodigal son to intervene and stop his son from making the foolish decision to leave home. Folks in town would not have talked nearly as much; however, the son would have missed one of the most important lessons in his life. It was far better that he was given an opportunity to see his need by a father who accepted the hardest job—not living his life through his son!

Following the Pattern

When we are tempted to overprotect children and develop dependency patterns in them we may think we are showing love. After all, didn't God give Himself to us in love? Don't we receive "every good and every perfect gift from Him" (see Jas. 1:17)? If this is what we think, we have seriously misread the Scriptures. The pattern laid out there is quite the opposite.

One of the key passages on this subject is found in the opening verses of Romans 5. In an interesting progression of words Paul reminds us that difficulty is not to be avoided at all costs. Actually, difficulty has a way of producing character in us!

I do not mean to imply that we intentionally go looking for trouble. I know one man who prayed that God would send him hard experiences so he could grow. I have always felt there were enough of those in the normal course of events without asking for more! However, we should also be careful that we do not always follow the path of least resistance. We should be particularly careful that we do not always shield children from difficulty—helping them find that path of least resistance.

The Scriptures are full of illustrations at this point. Take Daniel, for instance. There is good reason to believe that Daniel was still in his teen years when he was taken into captivity by the Babylonians. Obviously his family had little choice but to let him face that difficulty alone. They could not shield him from it even if they had wanted to. But was that a negative experience for him? Quite the opposite! Through that time of forced independence in the face of trouble Daniel was developing strength of character that would equip him for leadership.

Joseph is another interesting illustration. Every piece of evidence leads us to believe that he could easily be classified as an overprotected child. It was his status as the "favorite son" that created the tension existing between him and his brothers. Could Joseph develop into a leader if he remained in that setting? God apparently thought not. So Joseph was forcibly (would we say tragically?) put on his own. In Egypt there was no one to lovingly protect him from the hardships of life. But in that setting a new level of character was being developed and Joseph ultimately became a decisive, independent leader.

The story of Moses is similar. Here was a young man living in the pampered life-style of the Egyptian palace. Could he lead Israel if he remained in that context? Again, God evidently thought not. He sent Moses to the wilderness to face all the risks and hardships of that life-style. From that experience, though, came a leader—a leader who could face the challenge of leading two million people through the wilderness—a leader who could give decisive direction to this fledgling nation.

Peter should be added to the list. Under the loving eye of Christ Himself, Peter was allowed to fail in the courtyard of the Temple. The Lord did not bail him out of that tense moment even though He knew failure would be the final result. We may never fully appreciate though how important that lesson was in Peter's development as a leader as he learned the relationship between his weakness and his dependency on God.

The thread running through all these biblical illustrations is that love does not always shield from difficulty. Love knows that for adequate personal development it is necessary to learn by experience how to cope with hardship. When we fail to appreciate that important lesson we have discouraged the normal pattern of growth from which leaders can emerge!

What could be even worse is that by our overprotection we give children a false image of their heavenly Father. In our homes we as parents have a great deal to do with the way our children perceive God. Do we really want children to feel that God is in the business of always bailing them out of difficulty? Is it realistic to assume that discipline is inconsistent with love (see Heb. 12:10,11)? Surely there will come times when it is God's will that we learn to go *through* a situation rather than *around* it. Paul learned this with his "thorn in the flesh" which God chose not to remove. How will that kind of situation be handled by the child who has assumed from parental example that if God really loved him He would not let him endure difficulty?

Basically, then, the pattern of Scripture is one of development toward independent strength, not protection toward weakness. It is that pattern we must emphasize if we are to see leaders coming from our homes. It is that pattern which is involved in passing on the formula (how to face difficulty successfully) instead of the product (a life of ease and contentment).

Letting Go Gradually

Perhaps clarification is in order. There are those who might interpret the discussion to this point to mean that we should take our hands off our children and let them do as they please. That, however, is definitely not what I suggest!

To develop leaders without falling into the trap of overprotection does not eliminate the need for discipline. What we must recognize is that discipline should be a positive program of development for our children, not a negative reaction to their behavior after the fact. In our discipline we should seek to guide our children in developing an ability to make wise choices. That cannot be done without giving them real-life experience in growing dosages.

An article in *Eternity* magazine (April, 1977) said it well: "Maybe we need to see our task as helping people develop the skill of making proper choices. That skill will not be developed, either, if they make those choices only in a protected environment. If they grow up in a protected environment and then are turned loose 'cold turkey' upon the world, they will find it very hard to make proper choices because values are only internalized in the crucible of living experiences."

We should see this as a process of gradually letting go of the control of our children's lives. We never simply take our hands off of their lives completely, but we can let go of them a little bit at a time. It is a constant and careful balance between overloading them with decisions they can't handle on one side and denying them the privilege of personal development by making all their decisions on the other.

With growth, that balance should shift from dependence to independence. We might illustrate it this way:

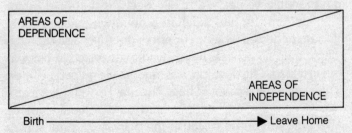

As the child grows older there will be more and more areas where his independence is not only recognized but encouraged. At birth we will, of course, shield the child from difficulty and danger. But if we are still doing that by the time that child leaves home, something has gone wrong!

Even the way we release our children to their own decision making is important. We can never dump problems on them; rather, our posture should be one of partnership. We can encourage and counsel a child as he faces decisions and problems. Our encouragement at those times will be invaluable as long as we do not violate their increasing right to independence.

There may even be times when we will have to force decision-making situations on our children to keep them from slipping into a dependence pattern. I recall a friend telling me of the time he took his boy to buy a new shirt. The boy's idea of choice was to get "whatever you and mom want." Finally the father gave him three minutes to pick a shirt! He literally walked away and forced the boy to make a decision. There was a father who wisely recognized the need to develop independent judgment in his child.

As we move through this process of development toward independence we will have to have great wisdom to know which issues a child is ready to tackle on his own. This is not always easy! Our daughter was faced with a decision regarding an activity which some would feel had questionable value. We finally decided that as a junior high student she had reached a point where she should decide for herself whether or not to go. All of a sudden the whole training process which we had invested in her was being tested. The decision was made—we gulped because it was not what we would have chosen. But after the event was over our daughter informed us she would not be attending any more because the activity was not fun or worthwhile. We were delighted, of course, with that decision. But, more importantly, we were delighted that it was *her* decision and not merely our decision forced on her.

So we have seen that if leaders are to come from our homes we must discover how to pass on the formula for life, not merely the product of our work. The absence of gradual development toward maturity will breed mediocrity. And that mediocrity is not the climate for leadership development. It will take wisdom to know how to pass on the formula instead of the product, but the reward will certainly justify the effort!

Six

Are Good Kids Good Leaders?

I was once told that until I was able to break the will of my children I would always have trouble with them. The person who told me that did it with straight-faced sincerity. So that I would fully understand what was meant by this advice, the self-appointed counselor went on to emphasize that children were not on their way to fitting in to life successfully until they had learned complete submission to authority. Until they learned to be good followers they could never earn the right to be good leaders.

For quite some time I confess I bought that concept. After all, it was reconfirmed by most of my experience. The churches I knew of consistently honored the young person who "fit in" best. Christian schools cast great suspicion on any student who was too much of a freethinker. To reinforce the danger of such freethinking, chapel messages reminded us that the biblical pattern of submission to authority meant learning to be happy with things *as they were* (*status quo* is the less honored phrase).

Lo and behold, the same lesson was reiterated as I entered the ministry. Denomination politics were such that asking questions was definitely discouraged. The spirit of unity was evidently fragile enough that willing agreement to the ideas of leaders was the only cement that could hold things together. Of course, the reward for being a good follower in that setting was a chance at being a leader someday! Be patient and work your way up. That was the rule in the thinking of many of those Christians.

What about all this? Can these ideas be supported in either Scripture or experience? Are there, perhaps, inherent weaknesses in such a philosophy? Almost by accident, one evening a former college buddy of mine got into a discussion with me regarding this matter. To our mutual amazement we discovered that a review of the roster of our college graduating class disproved that theory. With alarming consistency we discovered that those who were perceived to be the good students in college (meaning they did not question what they were told) often turned out to be capable of only average or less than average leadership ability. In fact, many of them had actually become spiritual dropouts along the way. By contrast a high percentage of our classmates who had consistently raised questions about what they were told in college (some would describe them as "troublemakers") went on to quickly assume leadership positions in various fields of endeavor.

Obviously, conclusions drawn from such a limited sampling lack scientific statistical support. However, subsequent conversations with other Christians whose experiences have been similar help confirm in my mind that we are on the right track when we raise serious questions concerning the virtue of "fitting in" as a prerequisite to leadership.

Are Leaders Followers First?

The basic question we must face is whether or not it is really true that leaders are followers first. Should we assume that qualification for leadership begins with an ability to work submissively under another leader?

Before going any further it is not our intention to confuse the matter of submission to God with the issue of submission to human authority. Of course we are to be submissive to God. This is, in fact, the genius of leadership. Human leaders are most effective when they have submitted to God's leadership. It is that very submission which gives them freedom to be independent leaders. Because they fear God, they need not fear men!

No better illustration of this can be found than in an incident in the life of Daniel (see Dan. 6). Daniel's determination to pray to God despite the decree that everyone should worship only the emperor puts on display a man who was free from the pressure to fit into human authority. Why? Because he was submissive to God's authority alone! His fear of God freed him from the fear of men.

Also it should be said that an attitude of not having to fit into human authority is not meant to be synonymous with rebellion. Rebellion carries with it a bitter, defiant spirit which is never characteristic of the serious Christian. But one can raise questions and challenge traditions with a view toward accomplishing greater feats than ever before without being guilty of rebellion. No one illustrates that fact better than Christ Himself. Without ever succumbing to a rebellious spirit, He still challenged the accepted traditions whenever necessary. After all, if there is to be new wine it must be put into new wineskins (see Luke 5:37). In other words, it is hard to receive new bursts of God's creative spirit if we are trapped by our old traditions.

With these disclaimers we return to the original question. Are leaders followers first? Even a cursory glance into Scripture begins to answer that question. What can we learn from people who were leaders in Bible history?

When God needed someone at the center of a plan to preserve His fledgling Jewish family during an impending famine He chose a somewhat cocky, independent young man named Joseph. Because Joseph did not fit in, even at home, he ended up on an odyssey that led him through desert pits, slavery, and prison, and after that almost instantly to a position of chief ruler in Egypt (see Gen. 37—41). His independent spirit and dependence on God were never watered down by being a follower "working his way up." Instead, he was possessed of a confident spirit which equipped him for imaginative leadership.

Moses was literally snatched from the Jewish system as a baby. So much a stranger was he to the structure of Jewish life that when he sought to intervene in a fight between two of his brethren he became the victim instead and had to flee for his life (see Exod. 2:13-15). But this unknown peacemaker later became the leader of over two million Jews. Shaped by God's leadership, not man's, Moses was selected to tackle a job for which he never "worked his way up the ladder."

David was a young man plucked out of the fields to become a king. He certainly did not fit into the régime of King Saul, but he was being uniquely prepared by God for significant leadership in Israel!

Nehemiah had no particular claim to fame. He was only a butler for a foreign emperor. However, when he was moved by the plight of his countrymen back in Jerusalem he sprang into leadership. He had to overcome years of depressed status quo (it is likely that Jews had lived among the ruins of Jerusalem without change for 90-100 years by the time Nehemiah arrived on the scene). But because he had not worked his way up some management ladder he was able to approach the problem of rebuilding Jerusalem with fresh ideas and hope. And what an accomplishment Nehemiah was able to inspire! In 52 days the walls were rebuilt (see Neh. 6:15)—something that had been left undone for decades.

In the New Testament the apostle Paul is the outstanding example of our principle. When God needed someone to lead the Christian missionary assault He did not choose a person from within the existing hierarchy of the church. Rather, He chose a rebel Jewish leader with a fiery spirit and unbounded energy. That sort of person could be harnessed by God to launch into an enterprise never before attempted.

Many other biblical names could be added to this list. And, of course, there were people who did work under another before assuming leadership (e.g., Elisha and his training from Elijah). But one cannot help but be struck by the repeated instances in which God chose significant leaders from outside the ranks of the established structures.

Interestingly, this observation has been confirmed in the business world. In the now famous book, *The Peter Principle*, the author disassociates himself from the idea that a good leader must first be a good follower. "You might as well say that the ability to float depends on the ability to sink."[12] Following and leading are two different functions. Followers may win some promotions, but that does not mean they will make good leaders.

Dr. Robert McMurry confirmed this idea in the November 1973 issue of the *Michigan Business Review*. He described the overdependent worker as one least likely to be advanced to leadership. Such an employee had pursued a career in a structured environment which required few risk-taking decisions. In describing this employee, McMurry goes on to say that "his performance was judged exclusively on the basis of his diligence, loyalty, and technical competence. *Docility was often favorably regarded*" (italics mine). That worker can be a good follower, but he is definitely a poor risk as a leader.

One can begin to see why it is so important to disavow ourselves of the idea that leaders must be followers first. What a tragic mistake it would be to take a person who shows promise of leadership and, because of a false notion, try to squeeze him into the mold of being a follower first. In that very act we could squelch the spark of creativity that could lead to leadership.

But Fitting in Is Easier!

Some years ago I spent a long evening talking with a pastor friend. He was terribly discouraged. As a friend I sought to listen to him and offer encouragement where I could. His discouragement did not stem from obstinate deacons, home disappointments, or the failure to pastor a large church. It came from weariness over having his ideas ignored. All his life he had held some ideas that ran counter to the denomination in which he ministered. Admittedly, some of those ideas were probably of little value (who of us does not have some ideas like that!). His biggest problem was that many of his ideas were ahead of their time. And for daring to think ahead this pastor had been ignored by those already in leadership. I honestly believe he was not as concerned about having his ideas accepted as he was having himself accepted for thinking them! But it was not to be.

In his discouragement, that pastor had reached the point where he no longer felt like fighting. For him the old commercial slogan was about to be reversed. He would rather "switch than fight." It was so much easier to fit in than to be different.

Any normal person wants acceptance. It is not wrong

to want to be loved. We were made to respond to positive reinforcement from others. For all too many of us that means we are susceptible to peer pressure to fit in. "Be one of the gang"; "Do what you are told"; "Learn to be a good team person." It is not hard to see how this pressure can kill the creativity that results in leadership. Like my pastor friend we reach a point where we simply refuse to assert ourselves at all for fear of being rejected again.

Pressure to conform can be especially devastating for our children. We should be careful how firmly we preach to our children the doctrine of "doing what you are told without asking questions." Most children in the average Christian home want to please their parents to begin with. If we add to that natural desire the additional burden of removing their right to ask questions or think for themselves we have done them a grave disservice.

I was positively impressed with a casual remark made by a mother recently. Her son had come home with a book that propounded a viewpoint in conflict with the standards of that family. However, when the son made the expected remark, "this book doesn't make sense," the mother made an unexpected remark. Instead of immediately agreeing (she did agree, by the way, that the book did not make sense) she asked her son what *his* reasons were for not liking the book: "You have to have reasons for what you think!" That piece of wisdom from a mother to her son was priceless. She was helping him avoid the easy road of merely fitting into his situation and was forcing him to think independent thoughts.

As parents (or church leaders) it is also easier for us if our children fit in. We, too, receive reinforcement from the comfortable status quo. There are very few fathers who would not feel good with a compliment about their "well-behaved children." That is not bad, of course! Unless, that is, such a statement is made because we have made obedient robots out of our children. It is not easy to have children who hold to ideas different from ours. In fact, it can be downright threatening! But can we really say it is fair to encourage our children to accept our ideas without questions just because it is easier for us? I think not!

What we are saying is simply that the path of least resistance is not necessarily the best. Just because parents and children may both find it easier to "fit in" rather than take uniquely individual paths in life does not mean fitting in is best. Even our Lord supported that principle when He spoke of a broad, easy way that leads to destruction and a hard, narrow way that leads to life (see Matt. 7:13,14). Yes, it is easier to fit in and think like everyone else. Being a follower has its distinct advantages. Obviously for some this is the Lord's way. But with the need we face for strategically placed leaders, let us not make the mistake of picturing the easy way as the preferred way. Rather, let us be prepared to encourage the unique individuality in our children and Christian friends from which leadership can grow.

The Hollow Victory

Anyone who lived through the turbulent '60s with the rock festivals, anti-war demonstrations, and hippie communes knows that such phenomena evoked varying responses from the so-called "straight" culture. That was a time of tremendous questioning for thousands of young people and adults. Admittedly some used those days as an excuse to vent their bitterness and hatred. But for many it was a genuine cry for a different set of values. Why be trapped with a materialism that cannot satisfy? Why put things above people? Why allow skin color and cultural background to separate us?

For many it was too much to take; the accepted patterns were being threatened. This movement needed to be ended in one way or another. Some tried to squelch it directly. Others ignored it and hoped it would go away. Sure enough, along came the '70s with a new wave of peace. Young people did not demonstrate as much. They began to dress in the accepted styles again. The war had ended so there were fewer causes about which to get excited. Life returned to "normal" again. The adult generation had won. But was it a victory in the long run? Was it good that youth lost some of its idealism? Was it good that serious questions about life were not raised as much anymore? Was it good that people quietly slipped into traditional patterns so easily?

It may be that we win a hollow victory when we succeed in getting people to fit into the status quo. There is a great danger that we may lose much more than we gain with such a victory. Especially is this true in the Christian world where that victory is often reinforced further by having spiritual worth attached to it.

In my work as a pastor I have often observed with disappointment the deadening effect of our hollow victory. Young people who should be asking questions to help them make truth exciting and personal are instead quietly accepting a secondhand spiritual experience. When asked why they believe anything, the answer is simply that "my church or my parents believe this way." Where there should be the excitement and vitality of a growing life, there is instead the boredom of a person that has stopped traveling the road of discovery. They are now content to "fit in."

The tragedy of this part of the hollow victory came home to me when I was invited to speak at a youth retreat several years ago. I had been duly warned by some friends that this group was from a church that had little spiritual life. There was no commitment to truth such as *we* knew in our church. They had not been indoctrinated with the truth like our young people. What I found, however, was most revealing. Upon arriving at the camp site, I was greeted by some of the most exciting young people I had ever met. They were full of life and questions (perhaps a combination that was not accidental). Never have I spoken to a group that was more eager to listen and interact with what I had to say. True, they had not been indoctrinated in the truth, but at least they had been encouraged to ask questions.

I could not help but compare that experience to the times I had spoken before "good church kids" whose interaction and curiosity had been squelched in the hollow victory. Those kids had been uninterested and bored with spiritual talk. They seemed to defy you to get them excited about anything. Is this really what we want? I think not!

The other tragic result of our hollow victory is the leadership vacuum it creates. If creativity and questions are discouraged, you can be sure leadership potential will be discouraged as well. We will succeed in raising children who do as they are told. The only problem is that we will have failed to produce people who can do the telling!

There will be leaders, though. If they are not produced in our homes and churches they will be produced somewhere else. And as we create the vacuum through our attempts to make people fit into our traditional molds, that vacuum will be filled by those who do not share our Christian ideals. Instead of Christian writers, teachers, politicians, and publishers, we will allow those who disregard God to fill those positions.

Then, despite our best efforts, we will discover that with disgusting regularity the leaders who do fill that vacuum will have more influence over our children than we do. The lyric of the latest song will be better known than the Scripture we thought we had taught. The values of the current television season will slowly chip away at the secondhand values we so carefully passed along to our children.

Is this overstating the case? Perhaps. But it may be true more often than we care to admit. The victory we win in producing docile children who give us no trouble may turn out to be more like a defeat.

That's Different—That's Good!

The positive side of the coin in the development of a climate for leadership is for us to encourage creativity and independent thinking in our children and friends. Without falling into the trap of saying that all change is good, we still must insist that openness to the new and different is the mindset from which creative leadership can come. Instead of a uniform mold for everyone to fit into we should be creating a climate where everyone has the freedom to discover God's unique mold for them.

The creative urge, after all, is God-given. Dorothy Sayers in a great essay, "The Image of God," points out that creativity may well be the point at which we come closest to the likeness of God. When God said in Genesis 1 that He was going to make man "in His image," we really know nothing about that image except that it was creative! That divine spark of creativity is what we must want to fan into the flame of leadership. [13]

We so often tend to think of discipline only in negative terms. Is it not logical to assume that discipline could also (and even preferably) be positive? Through a positive program of encouragement and instruction it is possible to draw out the potential possessed by our children. If we spent as much time giving positive reinforcement to creative bursts in our children as we do negative scolding for error, we might be surprised at the results.

I was reminded of this when my daughter had a slumber party to celebrate her thirteenth birthday. A short time before I had, frankly, been disappointed with her lack of planning when she had friends over. They had done little more than watch TV and talk. I was so bothered that I made a point of letting her know I did not like it. I confess I was surprised at the outstanding job she did planning that thirteenth birthday party. She kept the gang moving most of the night with planned games, craft projects, and snacks. Now came the rub! I suddenly realized that I had not even commented on this positive development. When my omission finally dawned on me, I corrected it quickly! I knew that positive reinforcement of that creative use of time would do much more to encourage her development than the scolding I had done earlier.

Instead of merely teaching children how to do things like everyone else we should encourage them to develop their own creative style. Rather than squelching questions with statements like "because I told you so" we might think of ways to encourage good questions. It is our task to look for ways to let people be unique rather than looking for ways to make them the same.

One of the kindest gifts God has given me is the friendship of an older pastor who supported and encouraged me during times in my life when I found I had to struggle against the "mold mentality." He would spend significant amounts of time with me as we talked about problems. I would share my frustrations and he would understand. As I worked through those issues that I felt were more a matter of cultural preference than biblical principle, he would encourage me—even when my choices did not agree with his! When I faced some major decisions in my ministry he urged me to consider all my options, not just the traditional ones. I sense something of the great debt I owe that man.

It is that sort of supportive encouragement that will result in leaders emerging from our homes and churches.

It is simply not true that leaders come from an atmosphere of docility. We cannot afford to be satisfied with raising "good kids," if by that we mean children who always fit into our preset, traditional molds. Our creative God wants us to encourage the tremendous reservoir of creativity that resides in each person. Ours must be a climate of openness and acceptance. Inevitably we will witness the development of significant leaders from that atmosphere. The bonus will be that we will have more exciting followers too!

Seven

The Freedom of Truth

Jesus made it very clear that we can experience freedom if we know the truth (see John 8:32). It goes without saying that effective leaders who serve to the glory of God must know this freedom. The stable qualities identified with leadership revolve around freedom—freedom from guilt, freedom from the bondage of men, freedom from ignorance, freedom from self-doubt, freedom from the paralysis of unclear goals. In God's Word we discover the principles that give us these freedoms. So the Christian who knows the truth should have an advantage in his preparation for leadership. He is, after all, committed to the truth that brings freedom!

Before we naively barge ahead, however, we should be honest enough to admit that the way we communicate this freeing truth to our physical and spiritual children can have a profound influence on the net result the truth has in their lives. Like any communication, the message can get garbled in its transmission. This lesson was illustrated to me again recently when friends of ours were coming to Chicago to spend a weekend with us. I had personally handwritten a note giving them the precise directions to our house. However, my handwriting was sufficiently deficient (others call it plainly abominable!) that the exit point on the expressway could not be read. After driving up and down the expressway looking for an unknown exit, they had to stop and ask for help. Even though I thought I had communicated the truth to them it was of no value because of problems in its transmission.

That is why, in creating a climate for leadership, it is as important to consider *how* we communicate as *what* we communicate. Is our approach one of indoctrination or introduction? At what point are questions welcome? Our need for a climate of leadership necessitates a good look at these questions.

Confidence in the Truth

Our goal is to see Christians entering a great variety of disciplines as leaders. One of the unique features that should characterize these leaders, since they are Christians, is their confidence in and commitment to the truth of God's Word. However, one has to suspect that it is possible to mouth a commitment to that truth while not really having confidence in it. Pressure from the Christian group can produce acquiescence. But that is not really what we want. How superior to have a commitment without having our fingers crossed at the same time.

Much of this confidence will be developed from the way truth is taught to a person. If truth is all tied up in a neat little package and presented as something to be accepted without question one wonders if even the teacher has confidence in it. Is the truth threatened by questions? If it is really true, can it not stand inspection?

I heard a statement made by a recent seminary graduate that genuinely bothered me. He said, "I'm glad I've been to seminary and know the truth now. It's nice not to have to read and study anymore!" There was a young man who would undoubtedly go to a congregation and suggest to them that they should just listen to him. They would not have to think for themselves since he knew the truth!

Many people, of course, take that authoritarian attitude toward truth because they know no other way to handle it. They were raised in that atmosphere and assume that this is the way it should be done. Others have less pure motives, for with indoctrination methods they are really grasping for power. As an authority figure they can dispense the truth to their subjects and stay in control. That way everyone is dependent on them for their understanding of the truth.

Churches and Christian schools are especially susceptible to authoritarian instruction. When seminary teachers teach from yellowed notes that have not been updated for years they are likely to produce pastors who are little more than parrots insisting that everyone agree with them. Questions are not only unwelcome but, in the eyes of these institutions, unnecessary. After all, they already have the truth.

All of this can have a devastating effect on children and their potential to become leaders. As I write this my mind goes to the stories of several people I know personally. The stories are so similar they can be compressed into one. This is the case study of Joe (or Jane) Christian, raised in what appeared to be a good Christian home. In that home he was expected to go to church and pay attention. Family devotions were a fairly common occurrence at home.

In his teen years Joe (Jane) began to raise some questions about the values he was being taught. That was when he was assured that questions are a sign of straying from the Lord and if he would repent and turn back to God his questions would disappear. At summer camp he did just that. And the questions disappeared—for a while anyway.

In every case the next chapter in our representative story leads to a Christian college. With relief the parents and friends of this young man sent him to the place where spiritual maturity was virtually insured. What happened, instead, was more indoctrination that ultimately raised more questions. Again he was told that he needed spiritual renewal, not answers!

At this point the stories start down separate paths, at least chronologically. Some Joe and Jane Christians made it through college; others did not. The dropout rate started with bright students who had real promise but became disgusted with a truth that could not be trusted. Those who made it through college began their service for God in their chosen professions. But as they entered the real world the questions increased. Never had anyone taught them how to have sufficient confidence in the truth to be able to handle questions. So, one by one, the dropout rate continued: some from the ministry into business; others from professions to cultic groups; others through broken marriages to lives of total disinterest in God.

In every case the root problem for Joe or Jane Christian was a lack of confidence in the truth. It was missing in their homes, their churches, and the schools they attended. It never had a chance to work in their own lives so, finally, they were overwhelmed by their unanswered questions.

The tragedy is that these are not hypothetical situations. Each case represents a real person who could have been a leader in his or her chosen field.

The greater our confidence in the truth, the less we will have to resort to pressure on others to accept it. Because we trust truth, and because we have confidence in the power of the Holy Spirit who is the teacher of truth, we will be able to present it to others with confidence. We will no longer need to be afraid of saying, "I don't know." And in our exciting search for truth we will never be too lazy to say, "I'll find out."

Truth is not subject to majority vote. It will stand on its own. Let us not suppose that truth depends on us to keep it from falling. Rather, we can personally search for it knowing that the honest seeker will find it (see Matt. 7:7,8). And we can start others, especially our own children, on the same sort of exciting search.

Gulping Down Guilt

When indoctrination becomes a substitute for confidence in the truth, a second dangerous corollary is likely to show up: guilt will be encouraged. When we are told that it is wrong to question what is being taught it is a very easy step to suggest that we should feel guilty about having those questions in the first place. The havoc that guilt motivation plays in the life of a person with leadership potential is enormous. A man or woman who otherwise could be productive and effective can be paralyzed by guilt feelings over unresolved questions.

The idea that guilt is an effective motivator certainly does not come from Scripture. Bruce Narramore and Bill Counts in their book, *Guilt and Freedom*, go so far as to say, "Not once does the Bible encourage believers in Jesus Christ to accept psychological guilt. . . . In the Christian's life, feelings of psychological guilt are always destructive."[14] The whole genius of the gospel is that Christ came to deal with our guilt so we can be motivated by a trusting love instead.

I called on a family one evening and we began to talk about this subject. This family had struggled with guilt motivation in their lives. Interestingly, it was a work situation that started them on the path to freedom. Jack told me of the plant superintendent where he worked who had just been fired. When that superintendent had first been hired, he came with a philosophy of managing by threat and guilt. No one felt secure. Everyone was watched for mistakes. The superintendent believed that workers would feel so guilty over lack of productivity that they would be inspired to correct their mistakes and work harder. Exactly the opposite happened! Productivity and quality dropped off dramatically. Jack said, "Pastor, you wouldn't believe what happened. In the time that this plant superintendent was there, productivity and quality dropped so severely that sales plummeted and the work force had to be cut from 3200 to 1300." It was left to a new superintendent to rebuild morale and inspire confidence in the workers again. That experience showed Jack how ineffective guilt motivation was.

When guilt is used as a motivation to learn truth the same reverse reaction takes place. Even if people finally give in and accept the truth through guilt motivation they will be depressed and unhappy people. They certainly are not candidates for leadership.

Does it not make sense that freedom-truth should be presented in a spirit of confidence and freedom rather than with a motivation of guilt?

The apostle Paul in Romans 7 and 8 presents a beautiful picture of the two ways to approach truth. In Romans 7 he describes his struggle as he wrestled with truth in the context of guilt. He knew what was right—he felt guilty for the things he was doing which contradicted the right—but he could not come to a resolution of the problem strictly through a legalistic emphasis on guilt. In fact, he finally reached the depth of depression when he described himself as a "wretched man" (Rom. 7:24). It was only when he discovered freedom through the truth (see Rom. 8:1) that the real process of growth could take place. In the security of this freeing truth he could develop a walk with God that led him to a place of leadership.

That still works! I will never forget the day I received a phone call from a wise father regarding his daughter. He recognized that something was very wrong in her life but could not put his finger on it. He knew she needed help. When Lori walked into my office she broke into uncontrollable sobbing. Finally she began to relate her story to me. Several years earlier she had struggled with a truth issue in her life. When she counseled with someone regarding her question she was put down for having the question. So she gave in and at least verbally agreed to the counselor's idea of what the truth should be. Little by little, however, the question returned. She faced a major decision in her life and decided to trust her judgment after all and defy what she had been taught. But that only resurrected the guilt. Had she forever ruined her chance for a satisfying relationship with God because she had not done as she was told? Her guilt convinced her she could not, and she was overwhelmed with depression as a result.

As we began to talk about the freedom of discovering truth for ourselves I could see a change taking place. "Your questions were not bad; they were honest. God is not impatient with you as the previous counselor was; He wants you to discover truth for yourself even through this difficult time. Your relationship to God does not depend on your ability to have all the answers to life anyway. It is based on the truth of God's love for you in Christ."

Seldom have I witnessed so quickly and clearly the freedom truth can bring. Lori's face shone as we prayed together. There were tears again, but this time they were tears of joy and relief. One person's search for truth was already bringing freedom from the paralysis of guilt.

If, as parents, pastors, and administrators, our goal is to

raise leaders who are free through the truth they are learning, the one motivation we will fear more than any other is guilt. We must have enough confidence in the truth to allow its freedom to break into each person's life unclouded by guilt. That fact has further implications which we now want to consider.

Welcome—Honest Skeptics

It was one of my seminary professors who first introduced me to the phrase "honest skeptics." He always insisted that he had no fear for such a person. As long as a person at least searches and asks questions there is reason to believe he will discover the real truth. What is to be feared is the skeptic who quits investigating. The closed mind is always more tragic than the questioning mind.

I suppose none of us enjoys being caught with a question we cannot answer. It is a blow to any parent, for instance, when his child comes home from school with questions about metrics or biology that stump him. After all, we are supposed to be the authorities! It could well be that factor as much as any which makes us discourage questions. But questions should not be seen as a threat to our pride; rather they should be the springboard to growth.

One of my favorite college teachers was a man who seemed to raise more questions than he answered. Time after time we would come to class sure that we had solved the problems posed in the previous class session only to have our neat answers exploded by a new set of questions. There were times when I wondered what that teacher believed. But I was not going to let his lack of sure beliefs affect me. I would leave class and go directly to the library to find those certain answers I was not getting in class! In retrospect, of course, I realize what that outstanding teacher was doing. He was forcing us to deal with the hard questions we would otherwise ignore. He was not content to merely recite truth to us. He knew that questions could be the exciting beginning of our own personal discovery of truth.

The beauty of questions is that they, in themselves, can guide us to the discovery of truth even when there is no formal instruction. Why, then, would we ever want to discourage questions? Early in my ministry I was invited by a friend to join a discussion group that met once a month. The format was that one member of the group would present a paper on a subject of his choosing then the group would discuss and question his subject. What made the group particularly interesting was the broad background of its participants. All were ministers but they ranged from strongly evangelical to devoutly liberal. There were Protestants and Catholics, Unitarians and Lutherans. No one was the teacher, but I learned. I learned because I was allowed the freedom to raise questions. I left those meetings more determined than ever to pursue answers. My confidence in the truth of God's Word grew as I discovered that it did have answers to the real questions being raised in the world.

This position is not easy for some people to accept. One day a member of my congregation told me that he did not want me to raise more questions; he did not come to church to have to think through issues for himself. He came to church to be given answers! I understood his problem as I got to know him better. Unfortunately, both of his children were going through deep rebellion against God. I am sure they had many unanswered questions. My guess is what that father was really saying to me was, "Why won't my kids just take my answers? I don't want to contradict traditional authority patterns; why should they?"

If only parents like that could see their children's questions as opportunities to lead them to discovery instead of seeing them as threats to their authority. Chances are we will not erase their questions by ignoring them anyway— they will ask them somewhere else! And they may ultimately ask people who are not committed to the values we seek to protect.

What a challenge we face to make the members of our homes and churches feel the freedom to ask their questions. We should hang the sign over our front doors and in the main entrances of our Christian institutions: "Welcome, Honest Skeptics!"

Let's Try Guided Discovery

We have already alluded to the path that can lead to truth that frees: it is the path of guided discovery. I would be the last to suggest that parents cannot have input into the lives of their children; children do not grow into leaders with a program of neglect! Of course we must lead them into truth if they are to be fully equipped for effective influence for God. That does not mean, however, that we must do it only by firm indoctrination. Better that we introduce people to the truth through guided discovery.

Recently the Christian education director of our church ran a series of weekend training sessions showing how to teach the Bible to various age groups from pre-school to adult. The common thread that ran through all of those sessions was the concept of guided discovery. Instead of merely reciting facts to students why not engage them in activities where they can discover truth for themselves?

Sitting through the weekend on teaching adults confirmed something I had suspected. The joy of learning is more in the excitement of discovery than in the sharing of results. As a pastor I had always felt that my learning was more enjoyable for me than for those who listened to me preach. The primary reason for that is that I have had the fun of searching for and discovering the truth. On Sunday morning I share the results of that search, but that is not the best part.

Fortunately, preaching is only one part of the ministry of sharing truth. Whether in the Sunday School class or in your own home you want to lead people in the joy of discovery. Obviously that means the parent or teacher will take the initiative in starting the learning process. But the wise teacher or parent will be a guide to the truth, not merely a dispenser of truth.

Harold Westing said it well in an April, 1977 *Eternity* article: "Teachers and workers must come to see themselves as guides and facilitators rather than authoritarian dispensers of religious instruction only." He goes on to reiterate the fact that God's Word will be a far more dynamic part in students' lives if they are taught how to discover truth for themselves.

As I mentioned earlier in this chapter, guided discovery, far from discouraging questions, actually encourages them. For children the key word is *curiosity*. A spirit of curiosity is the stuff of which learning is made. The "how" and "why" questions that we are sometimes tempted to ignore are really the exciting first cries of a learner. Just as curiosity leads to discovery when it comes to tinkering with things mechanical it also leads to discovering liberating truth. "Why did Grandma die?" "Why do we pray?" "How can I know God's will for my life?" The curiosity that seeks answers to those questions is our chief ally in guiding children to the discovery of truth.

This must have been what was behind the familiar instruction given by God to Israel in Deuteronomy 6:7-9. In those verses the Israelites were told to be personally committed to the truth. Not only that, they were also to teach this truth to their children. How they were to do it is what is most interesting, though. It was not through formal instruction, sending them to church, or putting them in a Christian school (none of which is necessarily bad). Rather it was by talking about the truth in real-life situations ("when you sit in the house, walk by the way, lie down and rise up"). Questions about truth can best be answered as curious children ask them from a context of life. Then a parent can guide children to discover how truth really works!

What a challenge we have in our homes and churches. A world waits for leaders who are possessed of a divine stability. That sort of stability will come from people who have been freed by the truth. Our challenge is to help guide our children and our fellow believers in an open search for that truth. We need not fear the questions that come up along the way because we have a firm confidence in the truth. In fact, we want to encourage questions that will lead to discovery.

If we succeed we will produce people who can lead with confidence. Truth discovered personally, you see, is a powerful motivation to action. Truth discovered personally is the path to true freedom. The way by which we challenge those around us to discover that truth will be a significant part of the climate for leadership!

Eight

As a Man Thinketh

Modern self-help lecturers are making a great deal of money today teaching a principle as old as Scripture. The principle is this: what we allow into our minds through our senses will, to a large extent, determine what we become. There are as many ways of saying that as there are ingenious promoters. But it always ends up being the same truth.

Some months ago a friend took me to an all-day seminar which promised to start us on our way to success. An impressive lineup of speakers greeted us that day and each one, of course, had his own unique way of presenting the theme of the day. We laughed and applauded and felt inspired. When it was all over, though, the several hours of lectures could have been boiled down to one theme: "What goes in is what comes out!" We cannot ultimately be something different from what we feed into our minds and think about.

John Stott puts it beautifully: "Self-control is primarily

mind-control. What we sow in our minds we reap in our actions." He goes on to say, "The kind of food our minds devour will determine the kind of person we become. Healthy minds have a healthy appetite. We must satisfy them with health-giving food and not with dangerous intellectual drugs and poisons."[15]

A manager of a large firm was talking with me one day about one of his supervisors. The supervisor had been hired because of his evident ability to deal successfully with problems. He had been put in charge of labor relations which definitely challenged his ability! But the optimistic and positive attitude which had characterized this man had suddenly gone sour. For some reason he was not able to keep on top of his work, and this was affecting not only him and his department but the entire organization as well. Some counseling revealed that the supervisor had been going through some serious marital problems. Literally every waking moment found him reflecting on the negative circumstances he was facing. His thoughts were completely pessimistic; there was no hope for reconciliation as far as he was concerned. That pessimistic mind-set not only soured his chance of solving his marriage problem but also obviously affected every part of his life.

One question that should be asked in pastoral counseling is: "What have you been reading lately?" I have done that on occasion with very remarkable results. With alarming consistency there has been a direct correlation between a person's reading and his problems.

In our effort to create a climate where leaders can be developed it is fairly evident that part of the battle will be in controlling what we allow into our minds. In our homes we will want to be certain that reading and listening material is uplifting and positive. In our churches we will need to challenge people with significant ideas and noble thoughts. We need to surround ourselves and those for whom we are responsible with a constant challenge to stretch our minds with ideas that build.

If we ignore this challenge we are doomed to fail in our goal of seeing leaders thrust into the world for God's glory. Pessimistic ideas and thoughts cannot produce optimistic leaders any more than pear trees can produce apples. Reading material that is restricted to issues of this world cannot produce spiritual leaders. What goes into our minds is what will come out!

Nothing New

Solomon was one of the first to put it so plainly: "As [a man] thinketh in his heart, so is he" (Prov. 23:7). In key teaching parts of Scripture that truth is repeated often. God has not ignored our minds. Our minds are not somehow unnecessary to growth. Quite the opposite is true. Our actions begin in our minds. If we can feed our minds with God's thoughts, we can succeed.

This was the main thrust of much of Christ's teaching. While the people of His day struggled to keep external laws and rituals, they failed to see where the issues of life really originated. They spoke of murder while Christ spoke of hatred. They spoke of adultery and Christ spoke of lust. They spoke of ritual, Jesus spoke of love. They spoke of an earthly kingdom, Jesus spoke of ruling their minds and hearts. Those issues have not changed.

Additional New Testament references testify to the fact that we are dealing with an old truth. In an earlier chapter we considered the tremendous eighth chapter of Romans which reveals the liberating dynamic of life that is freed from the struggle with externals. In our walk with the Spirit we discover new power to succeed in our spiritual lives. However, this glorious walk is not without our participation. Instead of our energies being expended in a human effort to obey law, though, they are directed to the proper feeding of our minds. To walk in the Spirit is to set our minds on the things of the Spirit (see Rom. 8:5). That means just what it says: What we read, listen to, look at, and think about had better include large doses of spiritual food if we are to succeed spiritually. That is how God wants to work—from the inside out.

As if to confirm this truth further, Paul gives more instruction later in the book of Romans. Recognizing the danger of being pressed into the mold of the world because of our necessary daily exposure to this world's philosophy Paul suggests the one way to succeed. "Be transformed," he says, *"by the renewing of your mind"* (12:2)! As God controls the thought life He can also control the whole life. That is not a new truth discovered by some modern management wizard; Paul knew it almost 2,000 years ago!

Paul's discovery in Romans is definitely not accidental. He really believed it. Perhaps his finest words on this subject are found in Philippians 4:8 in a magnificent list regarding the direction of our thought life: true, honorable, just, pure, lovely, gracious, excellent, full of praise. . . . Let those be the characteristics of what we read, listen to, look at, and think about. If it cannot pass that test we had better leave it alone! Stott comments on the quest for holiness as it relates to the mind: "The battle is nearly always won in the mind. It is by the renewal of our mind that our character and behavior become transformed. So Scripture calls us again and again to mental discipline in this respect."[16]

With a consistency that ought to catch our attention, great Christian leaders have been people who have guarded carefully what they allowed into their minds. Not only did they avoid the impure, they also avoided the irrelevant.

I was given a printed testimony which a Christian layman shared recently with a Chicago area congregation. In it he pointed to one decision which affected his life more than any other. It was a decision to spend one hour each day in Bible study, meditation and prayer. He felt that life-giving routine deserved at least as much time as he had been spending with the *Wall Street Journal* and his business journals. By his own testimony that decision not only revolutionized his spiritual life, it also made him a better businessman.

Often we hear or read stories like this and never have a chance to know if it really stands up under the scrutiny of day-to-day experience. I was particularly pleased when this story was confirmed in a conversation with another friend who happened to do business with the man giving the testimony. "You bet it is true!" was his comment. "That man has had a more profound effect on me and my company than anyone else I know. When he comes into our establishment on business there is instant respect." The old but profound biblical principle really does work: what goes into our lives will come out.

Realizing that we are dealing with an established principle like this demands our attention. Do we really want to see a flow of leaders coming from our homes and churches? If so, we must give serious attention to what is being fed into the minds of those potential leaders. Garbage can only produce more garbage. What we must do is find material of quality that will shape lives for God's glory.

To Lead We Must Learn

There is probably no area that demands as much from us all as does the control of what we allow into our minds. You see, the feeding of our minds with that which builds is a responsibility of all Christians, not only for leaders or those who are potential leaders. As all of us do a good job of mind feeding the climate will be right for some to emerge as leaders.

This responsibility is especially applicable in our homes. For parents to lead their children will mean that they too must be feeding their minds with positive material. They cannot afford a double standard. Being over 21 does not somehow qualify garbage material to become "adult." One well-known broadcaster refuses to refer to "adult" bookstores or magazines. He says they are simply dirty at any age!

It will be difficult, then, for parents with little self-discipline to encourage their children to fill their minds with worthwhile material. I remember meeting a couple one time who were very busy in the church. From all appearances this couple represented the best in good, solid Christians. After spending a few days in their home, however, I began to have second thoughts about my conclusion. I noted that the husband never read one page of anything except his material from work. There was no spiritual leadership that I could discern coming from that father to his children. The wife turned out to be a television freak. She watched all the soap operas, knew the names of actors to perfection, and had devoured every word of *TV Guide*. As I looked around the living room for reading material I found only a sports magazine to complement the TV magazine.

At the time that situation did not impress me, but now it does because I have been able to observe what has happened to the children from that family. With only one exception none of them has a healthy spiritual life. While all of them are employed, not one is in a leadership position. Is it any wonder that this would be the case when so little challenge was fed into their minds or their parents' minds?

Can we doubt the enormous influence we have on our

children? Jay Kesler mentions an important study done by Youth for Christ and the Department of Human Behavior at Michigan State University. A survey was taken of 40,000 teenagers to find out who the most important authority figures were for them, who molded their lives most significantly. Parents consistently showed up at the top of the list.[17]

Parents must never stop learning—their children are watching! And this learning business can be done. A visit to a good Christian bookstore will open up all sorts of possibilities for good reading and listening. Many excellent books and study manuals have now been put on cassette tapes for the person who prefers listening to reading. Your local public library can open up exciting new vistas of discovery.

If nothing else you can read to your children when they are young and with them as they get older. Perhaps a family journey through the Narnia Chronicles of C. S. Lewis or Tolkien's *The Hobbit* would be a starter. The point is that if we are to lead our children, we too must learn.

This discussion cannot be complete without a reference to the effect television is having on our ability to feed our minds properly. When authorities who have done studies on television viewing estimate that the average child will watch 14,000 hours of TV in his childhood, we have a tool with tremendous influence. Dr. Gerald Looney of the University of Arizona estimates that in his TV viewing the average child will have witnessed 18,000 murders by the time he is 14!

How can we get control of this massive influence? Obviously our minds are being affected and with them the potential for future development. The first point of control, of course, is the "off" button. There is nothing that forces us to watch TV! An increasing number of families are setting limits on both the time and the specific programs which may be watched. When time is up, the television goes off. Other families are building reading hours into their schedules just as regularly as they have viewing hours.

The television can be a positive tool also. Selective viewing can enhance our lives and better prepare our children for potential leadership. Public television often offers a good alternative to commercial programming. In some areas there are Christian stations available. News, documentaries, and good drama are also to be found at various times. The key is to study *in advance* what is going to be aired so that viewing can be selective.

Parents with some definite control over what they are feeding into their minds can guide their children in good choices, too. Parents who are still learning by their own good choices of reading, listening, and watching are more likely to challenge their children to be learners as well. And those parents are raising children who will be prime candidates for leadership in the future.

Attitudes Count Too

Feeding our minds for growth goes further than information gathering. It is true that there are facts to be learned in any area, including our walk with God. But that is not the complete goal for which we are looking. Another part of the mind-feeding process has to do with the attitudes on which we concentrate. We must not ask only what we *know* about life. We must also ask how we *feel* about life. Do we see life through positive or negative eyes? Are we hopeful or discouraged? Do we brood over problems or enjoy thinking of solutions?

Crises have a way of exposing the attitudes we have been developing. Any pastor, doctor, or nurse has had opportunity to observe that fact. Some people can recover from severe illnesses, or at least improve, not simply because they are strong physically but because their attitudes have been positive and strong.

I had the privilege of seeing that truth acted out in the coronary unit of a Chicago area hospital. The Johnson family had always been closely knit. They loved life. Family gatherings for them were the highlight of the year. They had developed attitudes that were positive. Now Dad was suffering from what seemed would be a heart attack too massive to whip. But this family was not about to give up. All their lives they had worked to approach life positively— why change now! There is no doubt in my mind that a family with bitter and negative attitudes would have lost their father from that heart attack. Not the Johnsons, however. Today Dad is recovered and still positive about life. That whole family persists in setting their minds on attitudes that build.

Aunt Effie Cooper was another person who had her mind set on positive attitudes. That is hard to do when you are in your 80s and have both legs in casts up to your hips from an automobile accident! Add to that the word from your doctor that you will never walk again. But that doctor had not counted on the healthy attitudes with which Aunt Effie would attack that problem. I will never forget the day when I walked into her home to visit and was greeted with a grin from ear to ear. Why? Because that day Aunt Effie had pulled herself out of her wheelchair and stood at the sink to do her own dishes. Yes, she walked again!

Of all people, should not Christians be the ones to set their minds on healthy attitudes? If we really believe that all things are working together for good for those who love God, and if we believe that we can do all things through the strength of Christ, the answer is yes. The apostle Paul certainly exemplified such a possibility when he described himself as "afflicted . . . but not crushed; perplexed, but not driven to despair; persecuted, but not forsaken; struck down, but not destroyed" (2 Cor. 4:8,9, *RSV*). That is genuine positive thinking in the midst of extreme situations!

We could go on to speak of other Christian attitudes like love, openness, patience, honesty, etc. All of these take cultivation. Perhaps that is why Scripture speaks so often about the lost art of meditation. As we set our minds on these God-honoring attitudes we will see the qualities of leadership rising to the surface in many people. We will also discover that such attitudes bear a striking resemblance to the fruit of the Spirit as described in Gal. 5:22,23! And at that point we have come full circle—you will recall that our discussion began earlier in this chapter with the idea of setting our mind on the things of the Spirit so we could "walk in the Spirit."

It is harder to measure attitudes than actions, of course. I can count the books I read and I can chart the television programs I watch. I can even mark down records and tapes I listen to. But how do I chart out attitudes which occupy my thinking?

Ultimately there are only two specific ways we can set our minds on positive attitudes. One is in prayer and meditation. There we can ask specifically for God-pleasing attitudes, and we can think through the implications of those attitudes while in a spirit of prayer. The second way is in the midst of real-life situations. We can develop patience on the crowded freeway, joy during the supper hour with our family, optimism as we pray with our mate for a special need, and hopefulness as we look at our child's report card. That is where we must trust God to help us fill our minds with attitudes that really count—attitudes that can be passed on to children and friends who possess the possibilities of leadership!

Getting Started

Leaders have to be familiar with ideas and gripped with the truth of those ideas. History is filled with the record of the influence of great ideas. No significant movement has been without an idea at its root. Leaders have fired their followers with that idea and marshalled support with it. Those ideas have not all been good, of course, but they have been effective.

As members of Christian homes and institutions we have the greatest of all ideas as the foundation for whatever we do. The redemption of men through Christ has as much to say to the artist and businessman as it does to the pastor or missionary. Christian truths are the mortar holding together a meaningful world view.

All of this is why it is so important to develop an atmosphere of curiosity about ideas in our homes. When we realize how great a relationship there is between what we think about and what we do we cannot ignore that thinking process. It is never too late to begin. Here are 10 preliminary suggestions that can serve as starter thoughts.

1. *Read Scripture together as a family.* You can purchase Bibles from the American Bible Society that are inexpensive enough to allow each member of the family to have his or her own copy. Read aloud (I think a modern version like *Today's English Version* is best) for the sheer practice of reading. Talk about ideas together as you meet them in Scripture.

2. *Find out what your children are reading at school.* Discuss with them the ideas presented in their school material. If you do not agree with those ideas, develop some good reasons. You may even want to read material along with them. By the way, we have found that our children have considerable latitude in the choice of much of the reading for book reports, etc. Help them pick good books to read!

3. *Establish a reading hour in your home.* This would be a specific time each day when the television goes off, the work stops, and everybody (yes, you too Mom and Dad!) reads.

4. *Visit a local Christian bookstore to look for books, records, and tapes that are of interest to each member of your family.* If you are not sure about selections, the manager of the store will be delighted to give you guidance. Be willing to make an investment in feeding good ideas into your children's minds. By the way, many areas have secondhand bookstores. You will be surprised what you can sometimes find in those stores at a reduced cost— all kinds of good literature, history, biography, and even Christian books.

5. *Make regular visits to the nearest public library.* If you do not have your own library card, get one! In fact you might consider getting one for each member of the family. In our area, school children are required to spend time getting acquainted with the library. Talk to your librarian if you feel you need help in making selections. Libraries are a vast reservoir of information for those who take the time to look. Make that library visit a family outing on a Saturday.

6. *Ask your pastor for suggestions.* Most pastors are "bookaholics" to begin with. They would be delighted to help you make good selections for all of your family. If your church is blessed with a good library, use it! Unfortunately, many church libraries are unused and out of date. Perhaps you could be the impetus to change that in your church. Since the church is one type of family there should be the same openness to think there as we hope for in our homes.

7. *Share ideas for reading, watching, and listening with your friends.* They may have heard or read something recently which would be of great interest to someone in your family. It could be that you can discuss with them

ideas you both have come across recently. Nothing will seal an idea in your mind like the opportunity to discuss it with someone. Some may want to go so far as to form an idea club where you would meet regularly to discuss a book, movie, tape, or TV program you all have shared.

8. *Consider offering incentives to your family if they have difficulty getting started on a reading program.* We do this in other areas, why not in the mind-feeding process, too? I know one father who offered his children a $10 addition to their savings accounts for every book report turned in to him.

9. *Specifically plan to get some motivational or self-help material to read.* There are a number of titles now available by Christian authors. You can find good books on motivation from management and sales-related sources as well. Encourage your children to do some reading in this area. Feed their minds with positive, optimistic thoughts.

10. *Consider watching at least one educational television program together as a family each week.* Then talk together about the ideas presented in that program. Find out why you agree or disagree with those ideas.

The best time to start any of these plans is now! If you have preschool children consider yourselves fortunate. It is generally accepted that children who have a foundation of familiarity with books, ideas, and conversation even before school have a distinct advantage. However, even if your children are older you can begin the love affair with ideas. It is true that we will tend to become what we think about. Our goal should be to fill our minds with noble thoughts. When that is the climate in our homes and churches you can be sure leaders are not far behind!

Nine

I've Got to Love Me

James Dobson, in one of the finest books in print today dealing with the challenge of raising children, makes this sobering statement: "I have observed that the vast majority of those between twelve and twenty years of age are bitterly disappointed with who they are and what they represent."[18] If that statement is even partially true in our Christian homes it is little wonder our children grow up with poor incentive to be leaders. I have to like me if I am to effectively lead others!

As long as we are still arguing with ourselves, the world, and God about who and what we are, we are not free to focus on other challenges. Life will be spent trying to defend or change ourselves. When our obsession is to "look inward" we can never get focused on what is all around us waiting to be changed by a person with vision. As long as Moses worried about his inability to speak and lead he had to stay in the wilderness. Only when God intervened miraculously to give him confidence could Moses become a leader of others.

To have self-love or self-confidence is not in opposition to confidence in God. We do not have to choose one or the other. In fact as we are submitted to God and dependent on Him we are most free to be at peace with ourselves. Our self-confidence can grow because of God's reassurance about who we are. Self-confidence without submission to God can produce a perfectly obnoxious person.

One of the most difficult people I ever had to work with fit the obnoxious category perfectly. He was a businessman who declared rather vocally that he was "born again"! It became increasingly apparent, however, that he wanted to use God instead of allowing God to use him. Without the evident spirit of dependence on God, his self-confidence became brashness. Like a bull in a china shop he roared in to do his work because he knew he was right and everyone else was wrong. The irony was that he was indeed very talented. But because his was a human self-love his effectiveness was seriously curtailed.

On the other hand, I am also reminded of a situation which reversed these factors with the same tragic result. This was a pastor who had certainly a deep commitment to and dependence on God. Absolutely no one would ever question his piety and sincerity. The only catch was that he had no confidence in himself. He was very quick to tell you how incapable he was. The result was a succession of disappointments. He pastored two fairly good-sized churches but failed to lead either of them to growth or renewal. Being even more convinced than ever that he was worthless he faded into an insignificant staff position in another church where little had to depend on him.

Somewhere in between these extremes is the truth. Good leaders are not at war with themselves or God. That means we must encourage both halves of that balance in our homes and churches if we are to produce leaders. God loves me so I have to love God, of course. But I also have to love me!

God's Special People

The biggest mistake we make in coming to an appreciation of ourselves is to measure our worth primarily by our behavior. Whether from the theological perspective, which looks at our sin, or the practical perspective, which looks at our day-by-day failure, we cannot have much encouragement with this view.

Some Christian leaders suggest that man's sin has ruined the image of God so completely that man is worthless. It is true of course that man is lost, but that certainly does not mean that man is a zero (to borrow a phrase from Francis Schaeffer). If God shared that pessimistic view of man we would not have been the recipients of grace. God saw worth in mankind. He saw enough to send Christ. And He did this not merely because redeemed men would be tools for Him to use but because He genuinely loved them.

I recall spending quite some time counseling with a young man named Rich about this very subject. He had been pretty thoroughly schooled in the idea that men were worth nothing. He felt we had no reason to talk about self-love because there was absolutely nothing in us worth loving. Our only hope for usefulness lay in the extent to which we become redeemed tools for God to use. What an unfortunate view! The overwhelming evidence of Scripture is that God loves us for who we are, not for what we do.

This mistake is understandable when seen against the backdrop of the world's standards. We live in a society where the biggest and best are honored. You do not drive across town to see a small house. You do not envy the fellow driving a small, inexpensive car. You do not copy methods used by the pastor of a small church. You do not tell your friends about the little office building you work in. If it is not functional or marketable it is worthless. Such a "success" orientation leads easily to the suggestion that for people, too, real worth comes only from successful achievement.

Modern educational philosophies often encourage this same idea. One current school of thought says that to be worthwhile means to engage in accepted behavior. My worth is not inherent then, but comes only as I perform to the satisfaction of those around me.

We need to realize that God wants to reverse this entire mistaken process. Instead of saying we must achieve in order to be worthwhile, God wants to assure us that we are worthwhile so we can then achieve. There is all the difference in the world between those two views!

I recall reading an account of a well-known college football coach whose son was a star member of his team. Someone commented one day how proud the father must be to have a son who was a star on his own team. His reply was that he was happy over his son's success at football. But he would be just as proud of him if he had never played the game. One has to believe that such loving confidence by a father had a great deal to do with the development of self-confidence in that son.

Jesus is not at war with our humanity. He does not see us as worthless, limited people. The glory of the incarnation is that God became a man. He did so because men were definitely worth a great deal to Him. They were worth enough to die for! If that is what God thinks about His special people, why then would we afflict ourselves with a poisonous, negative self-image that leads only to defeat and discouragement?

The basis then for a proper self-love is the realization that I am a special person in God's eyes. While driving on vacation one day our family saw a sign in front of a church that said it well: "You're a child of God, and that's somebody!" When I can accept that fact I can sense powerful motivation to grow. It will not be out of a desperate fear that unless I perform I will be worthless; rather it will be a response of love to the One who has encouraged me to believe I am worthwhile.

One of my favorite families to visit is the Baskin family. All of them are happy with life. They are alert to ideas. Without fail the children are high achievers in school. Mr. Baskin is a leader and I have no doubt his children will be leaders as well. Is it because they take advantage of learning opportunities with their comfortable income? Or perhaps is it simply that "brains run in the family"? Those may be factors of course, but I am convinced that the greatest factor is a genuine self-confidence possessed by each family member and fed by genuine love for one another as persons. More than once when I have commented on the achievement of one of the children the father will answer by saying, "Isn't he a great kid! He is such a joy to us. We couldn't ask for a finer son." There is a son who is loved more for who he is than for what he does. That is the stuff from which true self-confidence comes.

I believe that is exactly how God wants us to feel. As He looks at His children they need to hear Him say, "You're a great kid!" With that encouragement we can confidently move ahead to serve in a way that would not disappoint God's confidence in us. We will be driven to seek His help repeatedly. But we will expect that help because we are assured of His love instead of feeling we need to somehow earn that help by our good deeds. In effect we will become confident partners with our heavenly Father who loves us. I think this is exactly the balance Paul found as he said, "I can do all things through Christ" (Phil 4:13). What a beautiful balance between self-confidence and dependence from the lips of another one of God's special people.

Acting Like We Feel

The reason we must discover true self-love is that the way we feel about ourselves will have an enormous effect on how we function. This again is not some new discovery of modern psychology. Jesus said we should love our neighbor as we love ourselves. These words are recorded not just once in Scripture but repeatedly. The assumption is that we will love ourselves and that such love will be part of the foundation for loving others. When we are satisfied that there is something basically worthwhile about us we can invest worth in others as well.

By the same token if a person is struggling with his own sense of worth he will have difficulty attributing real worth to others. Can I honestly compliment the beauty in another if I feel ugly? Can I really rejoice in the accomplishment of someone else if I feel like a failure? Can I enjoy meaningful fellowship with someone else when I have great feelings of inferiority?

I was surprised one day with a long distance phone call from a friend in a neighboring state. "Don, what can you tell me about your friend Henry? We are seriously considering hiring him for an executive position in our firm." I had known Hank for many years and thought he was comfortably settled in a new job. Yes, my friend knew that Hank had not been in his new job all that long but he felt there might be interest in a change already. "We have gotten good reports from all his references. This guy really seems to have the abilities we need in our company."

I could not disagree regarding Hank's ability. But I did have some misgivings that had to be shared. Hank had expressed to me on more than one occasion feelings of inferiority. Though he did a good job in his work he felt inferior because of a lack of formal training in his specialty. He had learned by experience and had learned well. But the more he worked around others with college training the less confident he felt. To compensate for this inferiority complex he needed constant reassurance that he was doing a good job. In fact he had left a job only recently, largely because he did not feel appreciated. Now he wanted to move again.

Despite my warnings my friend went ahead and hired Hank. The chance to have a man with this experience in the firm was too good to pass up. Within six months Hank resigned! Being a part of a growing firm seemed attractive until he began to rub shoulders again with college trained men. The old feelings of inferiority returned and he quit.

I am sure Hank's story could be repeated more often than we care to admit. Our feelings about ourselves have a definite effect on our actions. Once we get down on ourselves it begins a vicious cycle. Our negative actions based on negative feelings tend to reinforce those feelings. We become prophets predicting our doom and then we turn around to fulfill our own prophecies.

Our feelings about ourselves in fact may have more to do with our success than our abilities. We tend to think that the difference between a strong leader and a lifetime follower is in ability or intelligence. It may well be that the real difference is in the power of self-confidence and self-realization. Your Josephs, Davids, and Daniels in Bible history had skills and abilities, that is true; but every one of those young men possessed a sense of self-worth and confidence without which their abilities would have been lost. They could face kings, wild animals, and warriors with a confidence that was rooted in a worth given by God.

We will miss the point if we send our children to school, give them private music lessons, have them work with tutors, and enroll them in special athletic programs, but fail to help them develop a proper self-love. All the skills in the world will not replace a sense of worth. The ultimate irony would be if our eagerness to help children learn skills actually became destructive: "You dumb kid, won't you ever catch on to how to do things?" We had better remember that wholesome attitudes about who we are will be more important than any skills we have because we will never act in contradiction to how we feel about ourselves.

Down With Proud Humility

About now someone is saying, "But where does humility fit into this picture?" My mind goes back to a dear old gentleman who talked a great deal about humility. Rather regularly in his prayers (especially in public) he would remind God of his humility. You could not be around him too long without finding out that he had prayed through the night recently . . . how his spirit was broken before God . . . how his own worth had been crucified with self. I really believe the old gentleman was pretty proud of his humility!

That could be a humorous story except for the tragic follow-up to it. Each of that man's children had evidently caught the same emptiness of proud humility and had decided he wanted no part of it. They all became spiritual dropouts.

What is humility, anyway? Admittedly Scripture warns us that we should not think more highly of ourselves than we ought to (see Rom. 12:3). It does not go on, however, to say that we should think more lowly of ourselves instead. What is being suggested is an accurate assessment of who we are. Humility is the ability to know both our strengths and weaknesses. With that balance we will never get carried away with our strengths because they will have to be seen against the backdrop of our accompanying weaknesses. However, we will also not be depressed over the weaknesses because we know we have strengths.

Humility is the check then that keeps us from getting carried away with ourselves. It does not demand that we belittle ourselves to do that, however. The passage in Romans 12 to which we referred goes on to encourage us to concentrate on the discovery and use of our strengths instead of concentrating on our weaknesses. You see, we do not have to possess great natural abilities to be worthwhile. We simply need to know what our strengths are and then use them.

It is a false sense of humility that keeps us from that. I have participated in an interesting experiment several times that illustrates this. The first time was in a seminar I attended where we were put into groups of four. One of our first assignments was to list five negative traits about ourselves and share them with the group. It was amazing to see how quickly and easily we all came up with those five traits. The next assignment was the hard one. You guessed it! List the five most outstanding things about yourself and share them with the group. Many of us were stopped dead in our tracks.

I have tried that same assignment on a number of church groups since that meeting and the reaction is always the same. We have somehow been sold the idea that humility eliminates the right to feel good about ourselves at all. What that tells us is that we need to be very careful how we handle the lives of those in our homes and churches. If our self-concepts are really that fragile we must treat them with care. Our goal had better be to build each other up. We do a good enough job of depreciating ourselves.

That must be why so much attention is given in the New Testament to our responsibility to build each other up. And if that cannot happen in our homes, it certainly is not likely to happen elsewhere. What are we doing to build the self-confidence of our children? How are we helping them evaluate their areas of strength? Are we leading them to a healthy self-love which will equip them to lead and love others?

I am impressed with Paul's definition of love in 1 Corinthians 13 and how it applies even to self-love. As a child of God—a special person in His eyes—I must be patient and kind with myself; I must not be boastful or work from the motivation of jealousy; I should avoid arrogance over my strengths; I can be free from the need to insist on my own way because I do not need the constant attention of others to feel special; I will not be resentful about my abilities and qualities; while I will not be happy with failure, I will be pleased with success; concerning myself, I will always believe the best, hope for the best, and strive for the best. This rather free translation of 1 Corinthians 13:4-6 could serve as an interesting basis for some further discussion in your home regarding self-worth.

Humility then is not an enemy of self-love but an ally. It keeps us from letting self-worth turn into carnal pride and it also forbids us the tendency to allow weaknesses to be turned into personality suicide. That good humility is what is needed in our homes if there is to be a climate from which leaders can emerge.

Establishing a Good Cycle

The beautiful part about the ministry of encouragement is that it begins a healthy cycle. The more we help build the self-confidence of our children, for instance, the easier it will be for them to do their best in life. As they succeed their self-confidence will increase. And on and on the cycle goes.

That also can work in reverse. We tend to look at some people (sometimes in our family) and assume they will not amount to much. With that judgment we then fail to give the sort of support that could help them to succeed. How superior a plan it would be to give special attention to the people who may appear to have less chance of success. To see that type of person develop a sense of self-worth that propels them to maximum use of their talents is especially gratifying.

My mind goes to Marty and Marie in that respect. I first met this couple when their severely retarded son was already in his early 20s. I knew they loved that child as much or more than any parent could love a child. It showed in everything they did. Even though the care of their son took a greater than normal amount of time they did it with joy. They were especially proud of the accomplishments of that son. I was amazed as I watched his development. The more they encouraged him and built him up the more he responded by increased productivity. The last time I saw this family I found that the son now was working part-time in a store—a feat which would have been unthinkable only a few years earlier. I have no doubt in my mind that such a dramatic result came because a cycle of encouragement had been started by sensitive parents.

Have you ever wondered how many apostles there would have been if we had been the selection and training committee? Could we have drawn confident leadership from raw material like Peter, James and John? The leadership of men like this happened because Jesus started the cycle of worth. He loved them as they were. He encouraged them in their growth. He corrected them without destroying their confidence. He forgave their failures. He expected the best from them. As that process was carried out, slowly but surely men were being prepared for leadership. Dependent as they were on the power of God, they were also confident in themselves because Jesus had shown confidence in them.

Starting that cycle is always worthwhile. While in the hospital for surgery I noted the dramatic effect such a cycle can have. My roommate in that hospital room was an older gentleman who faced very serious surgery. It did not take long to discover that he was a very bitter, cynical old man! I still remember his daughter apologizing to me for the conduct of her dad. "He has always been down on himself and hard to get along with," she said. I watched as nurse after nurse would leave the room totally frustrated over her inability to get this man to cooperate with her.

Then one day it happened. A nurse came in determined to make this man feel better about himself. Rather than scold him when he failed to cooperate she would praise him profusely when there was even the hint of cooperation. Through a steady diet of encouragement and praise I could see her succeeding where others had failed. Literally within one day's time that nurse accomplished more than all the others put together. She did it by beginning the cycle of encouragement. She made that obstinate old man feel good about himself—and it worked!

By the way, parents, this can work for us too. If we do not feel good about ourselves one therapy would be to help build up others in our family. We tend of course to do the opposite. When we feel inferior it seems to make us less patient with the imperfections of our children. That too develops into a cycle, but a very negative one. Our sense of worthlessness causes us to be critical of our children which in turn causes them to doubt their worth. The ensuing failure in their lives only confirms our sense of worthlessness. The cycle goes on.

But we can break that cycle with the positive one. As we consciously reinforce feelings of worth in our children we too will feel better about ourselves. And the better we feel about ourselves the more we can encourage our children. Self-love is as much caught as it is taught in our homes. It is contagious however, and once it starts it will spread. That is a disease we need more of!

A proper understanding then of self-love or self-confidence is essential to the development of leadership people. As part of God's family Christians have the perfect opportunity to develop such confidence with a proper perspective. Realizing that we are God's special people, loved by Him, we can honestly accept who we are. We will see strengths and weaknesses without false pride or false humility. We can appreciate ourselves as God made us. From that base can begin a cycle of encouragement and mutual upbuilding that will be another important part of the climate for leadership.

Ten

Show and Tell Time

"When all is said and done, more is said than done" is
how the old joke goes. All too often there is more truth
than fiction in that statement. We can talk (or write) all we
want to about the need to create a climate in which potential leaders can develop. Unless, however, we act on what
we know, our talking will be in vain. How much are we
prepared to *do* in order to create this climate?

As parents and church leaders the responsibility falls
directly on us. It is a twofold responsibility: We must, of
course, instruct our children in the areas at which we have
already looked; that instruction, however, must be supported by example. Unless we are striving for excellence it
will do little good to teach others that they should. If we are
not feeding our own minds with ideas that build, no
amount of instruction will lead others to do so. If we do not
have a clear focal point around which our lives revolve, we
should not be surprised if our children do not either.

In an earlier chapter we referred to Deuteronomy 6:6-

9 where Jewish parents were instructed by God to teach their children God's laws. In addition to formal teaching, though, they were also told to use everyday life as a teaching platform (when you sit in your house, when you walk by the way, when you lie down, when you rise). It was important to both show and tell the truth!

For those of us serious about seeing Christians enter positions of leadership in many vocations our job is clear. Both by example and instruction we must lead the way to develop attitudes that will create a climate conducive to leadership development.

Where Do I Start?

There are really two places to start leadership development. The most obvious is that we should start with the person closest to us—ourselves! As parents or church leaders it is always appropriate to reserve the hardest questions for ourselves. If we are struggling with issues of growth in our lives we had better give attention to those before we attempt to guide others.

This is not to suggest that we have to be perfect before we can help others. The flaw in that line of reasoning is apparent: When would we be perfect? It is legitimate, though, to be certain we have honestly begun our journey of growth before we seek to have others join us. In that respect we are leaders to others. We do not want to merely tell them where to go; we want to show them where we are going and invite them to join us.

One Saturday our family toured a local health center during one of their open houses. We were met by a very heavyset woman who offered to be our guide. I almost felt guilty making the poor woman go up and down steps. Her weight was obviously bothering her. You can imagine my surprise when she told us that she directed one of the conditioning classes at the center! I thought she must be kidding, but when I looked at the class schedule I discovered it was true. Unless she was a recent convert to exercise I have to doubt her effectiveness in teaching that class!

The second answer to our question is that we should begin at the point of greatest weakness. Failure inevitably strikes at that point. What attitudes do we find most difficult to work with? Those should be the ones we work on first. It is more comfortable, of course, to talk about those areas in which we have the least difficulty. Comfortable, perhaps, but not profitable!

The Lord had to stop me dead in my tracks on this issue when I preached a series of sermons on the fruit of the spirit. I discovered that study and preparation for the message on joy, for instance, was a delight. I could be eloquent on that subject since I generally have a sense of joy in my life. It was a different matter when I came to self-control, however. That was when it hit me. I wanted to avoid delving into that part of the fruit because it was the area of my greatest weakness. But it was exactly because of that that I needed to concentrate on self-control.

After that I decided to list the fruit of the spirit in order for *me*, starting with the area of greatest weakness as number one down to the last item which I felt was my greatest strength. When I finished that list I discovered I had a pretty good priority prayer list!

We should not be afraid to admit our areas of weakness. Instead, we should attack those areas first. This is real growth—turning weaknesses into strength. The excitement of such growth is what a climate of leadership is all about. And when we grow we will be equipped to lead others to the sort of growth that will produce leaders.

When Do I Start?

The flippant answer to When do I start? would be "yesterday." At best we do not have our children very

long. We need to make the best use of the time we do have
to put them in a climate conducive to leadership development.

What can be particularly frightening is that even in the
relatively short time we have children with us, we cannot
reasonably use all of it. As children grow older they will
increasingly be charting their own course. Whatever influence we have on them will need to come early in their
lives.

Many educators still believe that the first six years of a
child's life are the most crucial. The climate we create in
those initial formative years may well mold the direction of
the rest of that child's life. There are still too many young
couples who fail to grasp the importance of that fact. The
almost hidden philosophy seems to be that there will be
plenty of time to work with the kids when they grow up.
Such is not the case! In the era of the working mother and
the too busy father we need to be reminded of the crucial
nature of those first years.

Our children are a temporary trust from God at best.
There is a sense in which we begin letting go of them as
soon as we get them. That is hard for some to accept.
Perhaps if the idea of temporary custody really made
sense to us we would work harder to invest the best into
that time.

All of this is not to suggest that parents of older children
must accept defeat. Whenever we are in the parenting
process we can still profitably begin to create the climate
for leadership. It will be good for *us* in the first place and it
still has a tremendous chance of making an impression on
our children. We should never be so overwhelmed with
the odds that we quit trying.

One of my favorite Bible characters is Nehemiah.
When he was made aware of the problems that existed in
Jerusalem he could well have thrown his hands up in

despair and forgotten about it. But he didn't! Rather he decided to do what he could. He stepped out in faith and made a start. God honored that faith by allowing Nehemiah to see the completion of his dream sooner than even he could have imagined.

Maybe some reading this book are like Nehemiah. You may agree with the principles presented but in your home or church it seems to be a futile effort to even try to change it. Take courage! There is no better time to try than now. You just may be the "Nehemiah" in your situation to begin the development of a new climate of leadership development.

But It Takes Time

There is no doubt about it: to create this climate for leadership is going to demand time from us. It takes time to work a little harder with your child so he will do his best in his work. It takes time to allow your child the experience of doing things on his own, especially when you could do it yourself more quickly. It takes time to answer questions once you encourage children to ask them. It takes time to guide your child into a program of positive mind-feeding. It takes time to offer encouragement and patch up bruised egos. Yes, it takes time! But what is so important that it keeps us from taking the time?

A well-known minister tells how he was in a restaurant one evening having dinner with his family. A businessman who was a member of his church came into the same restaurant with some of his business associates. He swaggered up to the pastor and said, "I sure wish I had time to sit around with my family like this." The pastor disarmed him by saying, "My family is important enough to *make* time for a night like this. I hope yours is too!"

Even management studies are showing that workers perform better if supervisors show interest in them as

people. If that is true in a factory or office building how
much more is it true in our homes.

Chances are we will spend time in what we perceive to
be most important, and the time we spend must be with a
purpose. Since you have taken time to read this book in
the first place, further time could be spent profitably discussing the suggestions with your spouse, a group of
friends or a class at your church. Most of all, of course, you
should invest your time in implementing these ideas in
your home!

1. Invest your time in looking for ways to encourage
excellence in your children's lives. Take time to notice
when they do a good job and commend them for it. Point
them to examples of excellence—particularly to God
(chap. 2).

2. Invest your time in discovering what makes each
family member unique. Then encourage the development
of those unique interests and skills into areas of strength in
life (chap. 3).

3. Invest your time in giving a chance to each child to
develop a sense of purpose in life. Take time to talk about
it and then flesh it out in meaningful goals (chap. 4).

4. Invest your time in letting children learn through
doing—even when risk is involved. Resist the easy way of
"doing for them." Instead, let their own strength grow
through patient exposure to real responsibility (chap. 5).

5. Invest your time in giving positive reinforcement to
creativity. Don't dismiss the creative effort as wasted time
("Why didn't you do it the normal way to begin with?").
Allow creativity to flow even if it does take more time
(chap. 6).

6. Invest your time in exposing children to truth,
allowing them to question it, think about it, and finally
discover it for themselves. The shortcut is to make them
like parrots who repeat back what they were taught; but
this does not produce leaders (chap. 7).

7. Invest your time in feeding positive, lofty material into the minds of your family. Take time to read, talk, think and interact with ideas. The easy path of least resistance in mind development is bound to fail (chap. 8).

8. Finally, invest your time in building up one another! Never be too busy to share compliments, show love, and generally develop a sense of worth in your children. It will pay off (chap. 9).

This investment of time is important to the lives we hold in trust, and it is important to a world needing the influence of leaders who are Christian!

P.S. to Churches

While the major thrust of this book has been to parents and families I have tried to suggest from time to time that these principles affect the church as well. Every part of the climate for leadership development desperately needs to be supported in our churches if we take seriously our mandate to influence our world for God.

Some churches will find it hard to change attitudes that have built up over the years. It will take wise and courageous leaders to begin to move churches into the necessary paths of thinking for a new climate. But wouldn't it be tragic if we failed!

Some years ago I came across an incident that has an all too familiar ring to it. An extremely talented college professor was led to the Lord. He was a bright man with great possibilities both professionally and spiritually. His one fatal fault turned out to be that he did not fit into the evangelical culture mold. His background had not included church; he was not aware of our "unwritten rules." He asked questions about doctrine and practice. He raised questions about cultural habits. He evidently was not supposed to, for little by little he was squeezed out of the center of the church he attended. Finally he gave up and became a spiritual dropout.

It certainly does not have to be that way. Under God's leadership we can open up our churches to the factors that will encourage latent leadership to blossom. We can make a conscious effort to break tradition where necessary. We can do it if we sense the importance of the climate for leadership development.

For churches and church leaders, like parents, this will take time. But is that not more worthwhile than spending our time simply tending the status quo? We have a chance to be on the cutting edge of what God wants to do in the world. Perhaps it is yet possible to influence our world for God if we will create a climate that will produce a flow of leaders who are Christian. How exciting a church can be if we allow it to!

Not long ago, in a hospital seminar for doctors and clergymen, a panel of doctors and ministers commented on the joint role they must play in the care of the sick. What made the panel unique was that a Christian doctor gave the best sermon of the day. From his perspective he challenged ministers to their true calling in a way far superior to that which any minister could have done. In no uncertain terms he told every minister there that they had better deal seriously with the souls of the people they see in the hospital, for eternal issues were at stake!

That day I thanked God for a Christian home and church that produced a doctor who combined professional excellence with Christian witness. I was thankful for a leader—one who was influencing others for God because he spoke from that platform of leadership. May the number of those homes and churches multiply in these crucial days!

Notes

1. Francis A. Schaeffer, *Death in the City* (Downers Grove, IL: Inter-Varsity Press, 1969), p. 14.
2. John W. Gardner, *Excellence: Can We Be Equal and Excellent Too* (NY: Harper & Row Publishers, Inc., 1971), p. 3.
3. Rudolf Dreikurs, *The Challenge of Parenthood* (New York: Hawthorn Books, Inc., 1948), p. 125.
4. Leroy Eims, *Be the Leader You Were Meant to Be* (Wheaton: Victor Books, 1975), pp. 47, 48.
5. Ibid, p. 101.
6. William Glasser, *Reality Therapy* (New York: Harper & Row Publishers, Inc., 1965), p. 18.
7. Kenneth Gangel, *Competent to Lead: A Guide to Management in Christian Organizations* (Chicago: Moody Press, 1974), p. 125.
8. James L. Cooper, "You're a Better Leader than You Think," *Church Administration* (February, 1974), p. 11.
9. Francis A. Schaeffer, *No Little People* (Downers Grove, IL: Inter-Varsity Press, 1974), p. 259.
10. Jay Kesler, *Let's Succeed with Our Teenagers,* (Elgin, IL: David C. Cook Publishing, 1973), p. 27.
11. Bruce Narramore, *Help! I'm a Parent* (Grand Rapids: Zondervan Publishing House, 1972), p. 159.
12. Dr. Laurence J. Peter and Raymond Hull, *The Peter Principle: Why Things Always Go Wrong* (New York: William Morrow and Company, Inc., 1969), p. 53.
13. Dorothy Sayers, *The Mind of the Maker* (New York: Harper & Row Publishers, Inc., 1978).

14. Bruce Narramore and Bill Counts, *Freedom from Guilt,* originally *Guilt and Freedom* (Eugene, OR, Harvest House, 1976), p. 36.

15. John R. Stott, *Your Mind Matters* (Downers Grove, IL: Inter-Varsity Press, 1973), p. 41.

16. Ibid, p. 40.

17. Kesler, *Let's Succeed with Our Teenagers,* (Elgin, IL: David C. Cook Publishing, 1973), pp. 8, 9.

18. James Dobson, *Hide or Seek* (Old Tappan, NJ: Fleming H. Revell Co., 1974), p. 11.